Contents

Introduction

Modern web applications are often bloated and complex when they're implemented as full-blown client-server architectures. There are usually a frontend application, a backend application with a database, and an interface that lets both ends communicate with each other. In my other courses and books I teach about React.js for frontend applications, Node.js for backend applications with databases, and GraphQL or REST for the communication between them. Doing all of this yourself can be a lengthy endeavor though, so if you're looking for a stop-gap solution, Firebase offers a database, authentication, authorization and hosting by default to replace your entire backend application tech stack.

The React with Firebase application we'll build in this book offered a solid foundation for my own business for a long time. It also taught me the fundamentals of databases, authentication, and authorization from a frontend developer's perspective. Also I learned how a well-designed API has to look like in case I would ever design an API for a backend application myself. These are the main reasons I wanted to pass my understanding of React and Firebase along. If you choose to go with this minimal tech stack, you don't need to worry about a backend application yourself. Firebase takes care of it while you can spend more time implementing your frontend React application.

There are plenty of newcomers to React who are proficient with HTML, CSS, and JavaScript, who have learned React to build modern web applications, but haven't learned how to create backend applications for deeper business logic or how to connect a React application to a database. React itself can be sufficient for new JavaScript developers being frontend developers, so I often recommend Firebase, since it is a good foundation before learning more about backend applications and databases. It takes you a step closer to building full-stack applications, allowing you to build sophisticated applications with a minimalistic tech stack.

There are also the more experienced crowd who want to bootstrap their ideas as businesses. However, using only React may not be sufficient for an application that needs a database, authentication, authorization, and hosting. Essentially, some have the right ideas but lack the tools to create a MVP (Minimal Viable Product). After I published my initial Firebase in React tutorial, I heard many success stories from those who built successful businesses on top of it, so I wanted to offer this foundation for profitable business applications with React.

After Firebase was purchased by Google in 2014, it became even a more go-to tool to replace backend applications using authentication, authorization, database management, and hosting. In this book, you'll build a real world application with user management to power your ideas. You'll learn how to create a well-rounded authentication flow with sign in (login), sign up (registration) and sign out (logout). We'll also cover features to improve the UX like resetting and changing the password of authenticated users and social logins with Google, Facebook and Twitter. To prevent just anyone from being able to access the application, you will learn about authorization rules that protect certain areas of your web applications from non-authenticated users. You'll interact with Firebase's database to manage users and other entities, such as messages for a chat application, and learn how to structure data in Firebase's database and interact with it. Finally, you will be able to implement full-fledged web applications without worrying about a backend application or database using only React with Firebase.

Firebase is an ideal fit for transitioning to full-stack business application development. It comes with features you would otherwise have to implement yourself, and lets you experience how a well-built interface (API) should perform before you implement it yourself for a RESTful or GraphQL server application eventually. Firebase lets you focus on building well-rounded React applications using their APIs. My hope is that this book illustrates the enthusiasm I have for a minimalistic tech stack that lets you build large-scale applications without taking care about the backend application yourself.

About the Author

I am a German software and web engineer dedicated to learning and teaching programming in JavaScript. After obtaining my Master's Degree in computer science, I continued learning on my own. I gained experience from the startup world, where I used JavaScript intensively during both my professional life and spare time, which eventually led to a desire to teach others about these topics.

For a few years, I worked closely with an exceptional team of engineers at a company called Small Improvements, developing large scale applications. The company offered a SaaS product that enables customers to give feedback to businesses. This application was developed using JavaScript on its frontend, and Java as its backend. The first iteration of Small Improvements' frontend was written in Java with the Wicket Framework and jQuery. When the first generation of SPAs became popular, the company migrated to Angular 1.x for its frontend application. After using Angular for over two years, it became clear that Angular wasn't the best solution to work with state intense applications, so they made the jump to React and Redux. This enabled it to operate on a large scale successfully.

During my time in the company, I regularly wrote articles about web development on my website. I received great feedback from people learning from my articles which allowed me to improve my writing and teaching style. Article after article, I grew my ability to teach others. I felt that my first articles were packed with too much information, quite overwhelming for students, but I improved by focusing on one subject at a time.

Currently, I am a self-employed software engineer and educator. I find it a fulfilling pastime to see students thrive by giving them clear objectives and short feedback loops. You can find more information about me and ways to support and work with me on my website[1].

---

[1] https://www.robinwieruch.de/about

Requirements

To get the most out of this book, you should be familiar with the basics of web development, which includes knowledge of HTML, CSS and JavaScript. This article[2] mentions several things that should be kinda familiar regarding JavaScript before you start to read this book. You will also need to be familiar with the term API, which I explained here[3], because APIs are used frequently for the applications in this book.

Editor/Terminal or IDE

For the development environment, use a running editor/terminal (command line tool) or IDE with integrated terminal. Follow my setup guide[4] if you're unsure about which tools to use. The guide is set up for MacOS users, but you can find a Windows setup guide there as well.

Node and NPM

You will need to have node and npm[5] installed, which are used to run the applications we'll build and manage the libraries we'll use along the way. In this book, you will install external node packages via npm (node package manager). These node packages can be libraries or whole frameworks. You can verify which node and npm versions you have in the command line:

Command Line

```
node --version
*v10.11.0
npm --version
*v6.5.0
```

These are the versions used for this publication. If you don't see output in your terminal, you will need to install node and npm.

React

My other book, called The Road to learn React, teaches the fundamentals about React by building a real world application. It is available for free, and after having read it, you should possess all the understanding necessary to work with the application(s) from this book. Also there will be many sidenotes to React articles that may be helpful.

---

[2]https://www.robinwieruch.de/how-to-learn-framework/
[3]https://www.robinwieruch.de/what-is-an-api-javascript/
[4]https://www.robinwieruch.de/developer-setup/
[5]https://nodejs.org/en/

FAQ

Does the book use Firebase's Realtime Database or Firebase's Cloud Firestore?

This book uses Firebase's Realtime Database that comes with a free tier for experimentation and provides a good overall learning experience. Many online tutorials and guides are targeted at Firebase Realtime Database developers, because the Cloud Firestore is the newest version, so few guides cover it. However, migrating from Firebase's Realtime Database to Cloud Firestore is a straightforward process, as shown in this tutorial[6], which will be referenced at the end of this book again. To use Cloud Firestore instead of Firebase's Realtime Database, consult the tutorial to find a migration path. After you have learned to migrate Realtime Database to Cloud Firestore, you can use what you've learned from older tutorials that use the Realtime Database for your Firestore application. You will get the best out of both worlds.

How do I get updates?

I have two channels where I share updates about my content. You can subscribe to updates by email[7] or follow me on Twitter[8] to get updates more frequently. Regardless of the channel, my objective is to only share quality content. Once you receive a notification the book has changed, you can download a new version from my website[9].

How do I gain access to additional material from the course?

If you bought not only the book but a course that grants access to additional learning material, you should find it on your course dashboard[10] where all your courses and course details are displayed. If you bought the course somewhere else and not on my course platform, you can create an account on my course platform and find its Account Page to contact me with an email template. I can unlock the course for you after that.

Can I get a copy of the book if I bought it on Amazon?

If you bought the book on Amazon, you've likely noticed the book is also available on my website. Since I often use Amazon to monetize my free content, I thank you for your support, and invite you to sign up for my course platform[11]. Afterward, send me an email with the attached invoice and I can unlock the course. Then you can also download the latest ebook version on the course platform in case a new version of the book got published.

How can I get help while reading the book?

The book has a Slack Community[12] for people who want to follow along with fellow students and experienced readers. You can join the dedicated channel to get help or to help others. You might

---

[6]https://www.robinwieruch.de/react-firestore-tutorial
[7]https://www.getrevue.co/profile/rwieruch
[8]https://twitter.com/rwieruch
[9]https://www.robinwieruch.de/
[10]https://www.robinwieruch.de/
[11]https://www.robinwieruch.de/
[12]https://slack-the-road-to-learn-react.wieruch.com/

find that helping others to learn programming helps you internalize your own lessons. If there are no other options, you can always reach out to me.

Is there any troubleshoot area?

If you run into problems, please join the Slack Community. Also, check the open issues on GitHub[13] or the GitHub repositories for the applications you build to see if any problems/solutions are listed. If your problem wasn't mentioned, open a new issue where you explain your problem, maybe provide a screenshot, and offer more details such as book page, node version, operating system and the output of the stack trace for the bug.

What if I cannot afford the course?

If you cannot afford the complete course but want to learn about the topic, you can reach out to me. It could be that you are still a student, or that the course would be too expensive in your country. I want to support any cause to improve diversity in our culture of developers. If you belong to a minority, or are in an organization that supports diversity, please reach out to me.

Can I help to improve the content?

Yes, I would love to hear your feedback. You can open an issue on GitHub[14] and express improvements to the technical aspects or the text content. You can also open pull requests on GitHub to improve documents or project repositories.

How do I support the project?

If you find my lessons useful and would like to contribute, seek my website's About Page[15] for information about how to offer support. It is also very helpful for my readers to spread the word about how my books helped them, so others might discover ways to improve their web development skills. Contributing through any of the provided channels gives me the freedom to create in-depth courses, and to continue offering free material.

Is there a money back guarantee?

Yes, there is 100% money back guarantee for two months if you don't think it's a good fit. Please contact me directly to seek a refund.

What's the motivation behind your books?

It can be a struggle to find up-to-date resources about modern technology online, and the available resources often cover only a portion of a topic, so I wanted to help remedy that by teaching about web development completely and consistently. I hope to support the less fortunate by giving content for free, or giving back in other ways[16].

---

[13]https://github.com/the-road-to-react-with-firebase/the-road-to-react-with-firebase/issues
[14]https://github.com/the-road-to-react-with-firebase/the-road-to-react-with-firebase
[15]https://www.robinwieruch.de/about/
[16]https://www.robinwieruch.de/giving-back-by-learning-react/

How to read this Book

All my books are **not meant** to be comprehensive reference guides or in-depth reads about the technology itself. Instead, they are written as tutorials as you will find them online nowadays. However, most online tutorials are not consistent, often out-of-date, teach too many things at once, and never answer the *why* but only show off the *how*. I do my best to avoid these pitfalls in my books with the experience I gathered over the last years of writing technical content. You will be guided through building applications by typing out the code yourself, running into issues, and fixing them. You will learn about the *why* and not only the *how*. After you have finished this book and the application(s), you should feel comfortable in any source code related to the technology. This book is not only about reading it, but about getting your hands dirty. After all, I hope my books offer you the best practical introduction to a topic that is available as written content.

State of Flow

I reason that few people have learned to create source code from reading a book, and that programming is about the practical experience of conquering challenges and strengthening your development skills. Paradigms like functional programming and object-oriented programming require more extensive trial and error to use practically. Complex concepts like state management or control flow management used in modern web applications, libraries, and frameworks will take more than a weekend to master. These concepts can only be learned through consistent practice.

This book provides a more hands-on experience and challenges to help you grow as a software engineer. The challenges are meant to create a flow experience, a scenario where obstacles are met by your skills and tools. The idea is to keep the balance of challenging you and respecting your skill level so you can experience a state of flow[17].

Exercises

As mentioned, there are practical tasks in this book presented as exercises to fortify what you learned in previous sections. The tasks will include practical uses for the lessons, and deeper understanding of abstract content for your own projects. Most of the exercises come with the entire source code you have coded until then as well. Use this source code to track down bugs in case you ran into an issue in one of the sections.

Stepping Stones

Remember to internalize each lesson before you continue with the next section. The lessons build on the one before, and the difficulty of each topic scales horizontally using techniques side-by-side, and vertically using technique-on-technique. Its much easier to retain information if you take notes, so consider writing down questions that aren't covered in the text so you can look them up afterward. These notes can also become feedback, which I use to improve future versions.

---

[17]https://www.robinwieruch.de/lessons-learned-deep-work-flow/

Do It Yourself

I encourage you to write out code examples instead of copying and pasting them. Typing out code teaches how to find syntax errors and bugs, and you'll be better equipped fix errors once you've started trying the examples on your own. Don't get discouraged if you encounter bugs, as they usually appear in any application that is complex enough. It is acceptable to find them in learning scenarios because you'll have a chance to learn how to fix them.

Learn your Tools

These materials should be absorbed with an IDE or editor/terminal combination to type out the examples and observe the output. I provide additional tools that will support you with the implementation. Between the lessons, experiment with your applications and apply the tools you've acquired. After all, application is the only way to mastery.

Challenge

I write a lot about lessons I've learned, because learning and teaching has helped me a lot in my career. Continuing the cycle of teaching and learning is what we call progress. My challenge for you is to teach others while you are learning a new technology with this book:

- Write a blog about a topic from this book. Try not to copy and paste, but teach your own way to gain the most from the passage of information. Find your own words to explain the concepts, solve problems, and dive into every detail of each topic. Teach not only fills your knowledge gaps, it can open doors for your long-term career plans.
- If you're active on social media, consider sharing tricks you've learned in this book with friends. You can tweet tips about your latest interesting experiment, or show off your skills in web development Facebook groups or Reddit communities. Just be sure to take quality screenshots of your progress so viewers can follow along.
- Consider sharing videos while reading the book on Facebook Live, YouTube, or Twitch. Even if people don't follow your live sessions, you can always post the recording on YouTube afterward to maximize its exposure. Creating videos is also an effective way to verbalize your problem-solving process. If parts between recordings are taking longer, cut the video or use timelapse to show the highlights. Also, consider keeping bugs and mishaps in the videos, as these can be valuable learning tools for viewers who run into the same issues.

Application Setup

Let's get started with the React + Firebase application we are going to build together. The application should be the perfect starter project to realize your ideas. It should be possible to display information with React, to navigate from URL to URL with React Router and to store and retrieve data with Firebase. Also the application will have everything that's needed to register, login and logout users. In the end, you should be able to implement any feature on top of this application to create well-rounded React applications.

If you lack information on how to setup your React development environment, checkout these setup guides for MacOS[18] and Windows[19]. Now, there are two ways to begin with this application: either follow my guidance in this section; or find a starter project in this GitHub repository[20] and follow its installation instructions. This section will show how to set up the same project from scratch, whereas the starter project grants instant access without setting up the folder/file structure yourself.

The application we are going to build with React and Firebase will be set up with Facebook's official React boilerplate project, called create-react-app[21]. You can install it globally on the command line once, after which it becomes available whenever you need it.

Command Line

```
npm install -g create-react-app
```

After the installation, set up your project with it on the command line whereas the name for the project is up to you. Afterward, navigate on the command line into the project:

Command Line

```
create-react-app react-firebase-authentication
cd react-firebase-authentication
```

Now you have the following command on your command line to start your application. You can start your application and visit it in the browser:

---

[18]https://www.robinwieruch.de/react-js-macos-setup/
[19]https://www.robinwieruch.de/react-js-windows-setup/
[20]https://github.com/the-road-to-react-with-firebase/react-firebase-authentication-starter-kit
[21]https://github.com/facebookincubator/create-react-app

Command Line

```
npm start
```

Now we'll set up the project for our needs. First, get rid of the files from the boilerplate React project, since we won't be using them. From the command line, head to your *src/* folder and execute it:

Command Line

```
cd src
rm App.js App.test.js App.css logo.svg
```

Second, create a *components/* folder in your application's *src/* folder on the command line. This is where all your components will be implemented. Also, the App component that you have removed in the previous step will be recreated here:

Command Line

```
mkdir components
```

Create a dedicated folder for each component we will implement for this application. For the sake of readability, I split up the commands into multiple lines:

Command Line

```
cd components
mkdir Account Admin App Home Landing SignIn SignOut SignUp
mkdir Navigation PasswordChange PasswordForget
mkdir Session Firebase
```

In each folder, create an *index.js* file for the component. Navigate into a folder, create the file, and navigate out again. Repeat these steps for every component. You can choose to name your folders/files differently, but that's how I liked to do it for my applications.

Command Line

```
cd App
touch index.js
cd ..
```

Next, implement a basic React component for each file you created. For the App component in *src/components/App/index.js*, it could look like the following:

src/components/App/index.js

```
import React from 'react';

const App = () => (
  <div>
    <h1>App</h1>
  </div>
);

export default App;
```

Fix the relative path to the App component in the *src/index.js* file. Since you have moved the App component to the *src/components* folder, you need to add the */components* subpath to it.

src/index.js

```
import React from 'react';
import ReactDOM from 'react-dom';

import './index.css';
import * as serviceWorker from './serviceWorker';

import App from './components/App';

ReactDOM.render(<App />, document.getElementById('root'));

serviceWorker.unregister();
```

Then, create one more folder in your *src/* folder:

Command Line

```
mkdir constants
```

The folder should be located next to *src/components/*. Move into *src/constants/* and create two files for the application's routing and roles management later:

Command Line

```
cd constants
touch routes.js roles.js
cd ..
```

The application with its folders and files is set up, and you can verify this by running it on the command line and accessing it through a browser. Check the starter project on GitHub I linked in the beginning of this section to verify whether you have set up everything properly.

Exercises:

- Familiarize yourself with the folder structure of a project.
- Optionally, introduce a test for your App component and test the application.
- Optionally, introduce CSS Modules[22], SASS[23] or Styled Components[24] and style the application.
- Optionally, introduce Git and keep track of your changes by having your project on GitHub[25].

---

[22]https://www.robinwieruch.de/create-react-app-css-modules/
[23]https://www.robinwieruch.de/create-react-app-with-sass-support/
[24]https://www.styled-components.com
[25]https://www.robinwieruch.de/git-essential-commands/

React Router in React

Since we are building a larger application in the following sections, it would be great to have a couple of pages (e.g. landing page, account page, admin page, sign up page, sign in page) to split the application into multiple URLs (e.g. /landing, /account, /admin). These URLs or subpaths of a domain are called routes in a client-side web application. Let's implement the routing with React Router[26] before we dive into Firebase for the realtime database and authentication/authorization. If you haven't used React Router before, it should be straightforward to pick up the basics throughout building this application.

The application should have multiple routes. For instance, a user should be able to visit a public landing page, and also use sign up and sign in pages to enter the application as an authenticated user. If a user is authenticated, it is possible to visit protected pages like account or admin pages whereas the latter is only accessible by authenticated users with an admin role. You can consolidate all the routes of your application in a well-defined *src/constants/routes.js* constants file:

src/constants/routes.js

```
export const LANDING = '/';
export const SIGN_UP = '/signup';
export const SIGN_IN = '/signin';
export const HOME = '/home';
export const ACCOUNT = '/account';
export const ADMIN = '/admin';
export const PASSWORD_FORGET = '/pw-forget';
```

Each route represents a page in your application. For instance, the sign up page should be reachable in development mode via *http://localhost:3000/signup* and in production mode via *http://yourdomain/signup*.

First, you will have a **sign up page** (register page) and a **sign in page** (login page). You can take any web application as the blueprint to structure these routes for a well-rounded authentication experience. Take the following scenario: A user visits your web application, is convinced by your service, and finds the button in the top-level navigation to sign in to your application. But the user has no account yet, so a sign up button is presented as an alternative on the sign in page.

---

[26]https://github.com/ReactTraining/react-router

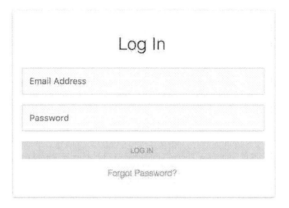

Second, there will be a **landing page** and a **home page**. The landing page is your default route (e.g. *http://yourdomain/*). That's the place where a user ends up when visiting your web application. The user doesn't need to be authenticated to go this route. On the other hand, the home page is a **protected route**, which users can only access if they have been authenticated. You will implement the protection of the route using authorization mechanisms for this application.

Third, next to the **home page**, there will be protected **account page** and **admin page** as well. On the account page, a user can reset or change a password. It is secured by authorization as well, so it is only reachable for authenticated users. On the admin page, a user authorized as admin will be able to manage this application's users. The admin page is protected on a more fine-grained level, because it is only accessible for authenticated admin users.

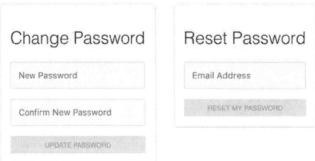

Lastly, the **password forget** component will be exposed on another non-protected page, a **password forget page**, as well. It is used for users who are not authenticated and forgot about their password.

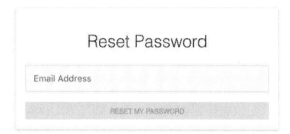

We've completed the routes for this React with Firebase application. I find it exciting to build a well-rounded application with you, because it can be used as a boilerplate project that gives you authentication, authorization, and a database. These are foundational pillars for any web-based application.

Now, all these routes need to be accessible to the user. First, you need a router for your web application, which is responsible to map routes to React components. React Router is a popular package to enable routing, so install it on the command line:

Command Line

```
npm install react-router-dom
```

The best way to start is implementing a Navigation component that will be used in the App component. The App component is the perfect place to render the Navigation component, because it always renders the Navigation component but replaces the other components (pages) based on the routes. Basically, the App component is the container where all your fixed components are going (e.g. navigation bar, side bar, footer), but also your components that are displayed depending on the route in the URL (e.g. account page, login page, password forget page).

First, the App component will use the Navigation component that is not implemented yet. Also, it uses the Router component provided by React Router. The Router makes it possible to navigate from URL-to-URL on the client-side application without another request to a web server for every route change. The application is only fetched once from a web server, after which all routing is done on the client-side with React Router.

src/components/App/index.js

```
import React from 'react';
import { BrowserRouter as Router } from 'react-router-dom';

import Navigation from '../Navigation';

const App = () => (
  <Router>
    <Navigation />
  </Router>
);

export default App;
```

Second, implement the Navigation component. It uses the Link component of React Router to enable navigation to different routes. These routes were defined previously in your constants file. Let's import all of them and give every Link component a specific route.

src/components/Navigation/index.js

```
import React from 'react';
import { Link } from 'react-router-dom';

import * as ROUTES from '../../constants/routes';

const Navigation = () => (
  <div>
    <ul>
      <li>
        <Link to={ROUTES.SIGN_IN}>Sign In</Link>
      </li>
      <li>
        <Link to={ROUTES.LANDING}>Landing</Link>
      </li>
      <li>
        <Link to={ROUTES.HOME}>Home</Link>
      </li>
      <li>
        <Link to={ROUTES.ACCOUNT}>Account</Link>
      </li>
      <li>
        <Link to={ROUTES.ADMIN}>Admin</Link>
      </li>
```

```
      </ul>
    </div>
  );


export default Navigation;
```

Now, run your application again and verify that the links show up in your browser, and that once you click a link, the URL changes. Notice that even though the URL changes, the displayed content doesn't change. The navigation is only there to enable navigation through your application. But no one knows what to render on each route. That's where the *route to component* mapping comes in. In your App component, you can specify which components should show up according to corresponding routes with the help of the Route component from React Router.

src/components/App/index.js

```
import React from 'react';
import {
  BrowserRouter as Router,
  Route,
} from 'react-router-dom';

import Navigation from '../Navigation';
import LandingPage from '../Landing';
import SignUpPage from '../SignUp';
import SignInPage from '../SignIn';
import PasswordForgetPage from '../PasswordForget';
import HomePage from '../Home';
import AccountPage from '../Account';
import AdminPage from '../Admin';

import * as ROUTES from '../../constants/routes';

const App = () => (
  <Router>
    <div>
      <Navigation />

      <hr />

      <Route exact path={ROUTES.LANDING} component={LandingPage} />
      <Route path={ROUTES.SIGN_UP} component={SignUpPage} />
      <Route path={ROUTES.SIGN_IN} component={SignInPage} />
      <Route path={ROUTES.PASSWORD_FORGET} component={PasswordForgetPage} />
```

```
      <Route path={ROUTES.HOME} component={HomePage} />
      <Route path={ROUTES.ACCOUNT} component={AccountPage} />
      <Route path={ROUTES.ADMIN} component={AdminPage} />
    </div>
  </Router>
);
```

```
export default App;
```

If a route matches a path prop, the respective component will be displayed; thus, all the page components in the App component are exchangeable by changing the route, but the Navigation component stays fixed independently of any route changes. This is how you enable a static frame with various components (e.g. Navigation) around your dynamic pages driven by routes. It's all made possible by React's powerful composition[27].

Previously, you created basic components for each page component used by our routes. Now you should be able to start the application again. When you click through the links in the Navigation component, the displayed page component should change according to the URL. The routes for the PasswordForget and SignUp components are not used in the Navigation component, but will be defined elsewhere later. For now, you have successfully implemented fundamental routing for this application.

Exercises:

- Learn more about React Router[28]
- Confirm your source code for the last section[29]

---

[27]https://www.robinwieruch.de/react-component-composition/
[28]https://reacttraining.com/react-router/web/guides/quick-start
[29]http://bit.ly/2VmQnNi

Firebase

The main focus here is using Firebase in React for the application we'll build together. Firebase, bought by Google in 2014, enables realtime databases, extensive authentication and authorization, and even for deployment. You can build real-world applications with React and Firebase without worrying about implementing a backend application. All the things a backend application would handle, like authentication and a database, is handled by Firebase. Many businesses use React and Firebase to power their applications, as it is the ultimate combination to launch an MVP[30].

To start, sign up on the official Firebase website[31]. After you have created a Firebase account, you should be able to create projects and be granted access to the project dashboard. We'll begin by creating a project for this application on their platform whereas the project can have any name. In the case of this application, run it on the free pricing plan. If you want to scale your application later, you can change the plan. Follow this visual Firebase setup and introduction guide[32] to learn more about Firebase's dashboard and features. It would also give you first guidelines on how to acivate Firebase's Realtime Database instead of Firebase's Cloud Firestore.

Next, find the project's configuration in the settings on your project's dashboard. There, you'll have access to all the necessary information: secrets, keys, ids and other details to set up your application. Copy these in the next step to your React application.

---

[30]https://en.wikipedia.org/wiki/Minimum_viable_product
[31]https://firebase.google.com/
[32]https://www.robinwieruch.de/firebase-tutorial

Add Firebase to your web app   ✕

Copy and paste the snippet below at the bottom of your HTML, before other `script` tags.

```html
<script src="https://www.gstatic.com/firebasejs/4.7.0/firebase.js"></script>
<script>
  // Initialize Firebase
  var config = {
    apiKey: my-api-key,
    authDomain: "my-app-name.firebaseapp.com",
    databaseURL: "https://my-app-name.firebaseio.com",
    projectId: "my-app-name",
    storageBucket: "my-app-name.appspot.com",
    messagingSenderId: "999999999999"
  };
  firebase.initializeApp(config);
</script>
```

COPY

Check these resources to learn more about Firebase for web apps:

Get Started with Firebase for Web Apps [↗]

Firebase Web SDK API Reference [↗]

Firebase Web Samples [↗]

Sometimes the Firebase website doesn't make it easy to find this page. Since it's moved around with every iteration of the website, I cannot give you any clear advice where to find it on your dashboard. This is an opportunity to familiarize yourself with Firebase project's dashboard while you search for the configuration.

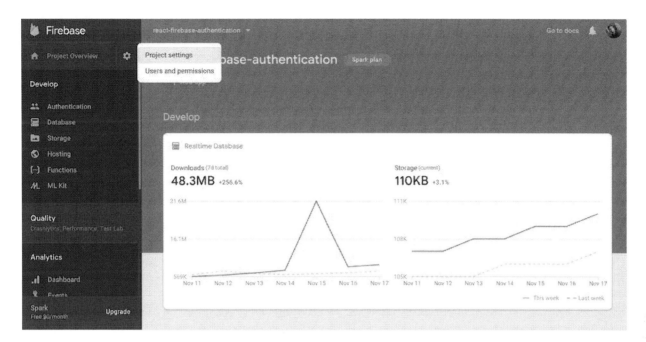

Now that we've completed the Firebase setup, you can return to your application in your editor/IDE to add the Firebase configuration. First, install Firebase for your application on the command line:

Command Line

```
npm install firebase
```

Next, we'll create a new file for the Firebase setup. We will use a JavaScript class to encapsulate all Firebase functionalities, realtime database, and authentication, as a well-defined API for the rest of the application. You need only instantiate the class once, after which it can use it then to interact with the Firebase API, your custom Firebase interface.

Let's start by copying the configuration from your Firebase project's dashboard on their website to your application as a configuration object in a new *src/components/Firebase/firebase.js* file. Make sure to replace the capitalized keys with the corresponding keys from your copied configuration:

src/components/Firebase/firebase.js

```
const config = {
  apiKey: YOUR_API_KEY,
  authDomain: YOUR_AUTH_DOMAIN,
  databaseURL: YOUR_DATABASE_URL,
  projectId: YOUR_PROJECT_ID,
  storageBucket: '',
  messagingSenderId: YOUR_MESSAGING_SENDER_ID,
};
```

As alternative, you can also use environment variables in React applications, but you have to use the REACT_APP prefix when you use create-react-app to set up the application:

src/components/Firebase/firebase.js

```
const config = {
  apiKey: process.env.REACT_APP_API_KEY,
  authDomain: process.env.REACT_APP_AUTH_DOMAIN,
  databaseURL: process.env.REACT_APP_DATABASE_URL,
  projectId: process.env.REACT_APP_PROJECT_ID,
  storageBucket: process.env.REACT_APP_STORAGE_BUCKET,
  messagingSenderId: process.env.REACT_APP_MESSAGING_SENDER_ID,
};
```

Now you can define the environmental variables in a new *.env* file in your project's root folder. The *.env* file can also be added to your *.gitginore* file (in case you are using git), so your Firebase credentials are not exposed publicly on a platform like GitHub.

.env

```
REACT_APP_API_KEY=XXXXxxxx
REACT_APP_AUTH_DOMAIN=xxxxXXXX.firebaseapp.com
REACT_APP_DATABASE_URL=https://xxxXXXX.firebaseio.com
REACT_APP_PROJECT_ID=xxxxXXXX
REACT_APP_STORAGE_BUCKET=xxxxXXXX.appspot.com
REACT_APP_MESSAGING_SENDER_ID=xxxxXXXX
```

Both ways work. You can define the configuration inline in source code or as environment variables. Environmental variables are more secure, and should be used when uploading your project to a version control system like git, though we will be continuing with the Firebase setup. Import firebase from the library you installed earlier, and then use it within a new Firebase class to initialize firebase with the configuration:

src/components/Firebase/firebase.js

```
import app from 'firebase/app';

const config = {
  apiKey: process.env.REACT_APP_API_KEY,
  authDomain: process.env.REACT_APP_AUTH_DOMAIN,
  databaseURL: process.env.REACT_APP_DATABASE_URL,
  projectId: process.env.REACT_APP_PROJECT_ID,
  storageBucket: process.env.REACT_APP_STORAGE_BUCKET,
  messagingSenderId: process.env.REACT_APP_MESSAGING_SENDER_ID,
};

class Firebase {
```

```
  constructor() {
    app.initializeApp(config);
  }
}


export default Firebase;
```

That's all that is needed for a firebase configuration in your application. Optionally, you can create a second Firebase project on the Firebase website to have one project for your development environment and one project for your production environment. That way, you never mix data in the Firebase database in development mode with data from your deployed application (production mode). If you decide to create projects for both environments, use the two configuration objects in your Firebase setup and decide which one you take depending on the development/production environment:

src/components/Firebase/firebase.js

```
import app from 'firebase/app';

const prodConfig = {
  apiKey: process.env.REACT_APP_PROD_API_KEY,
  authDomain: process.env.REACT_APP_PROD_AUTH_DOMAIN,
  databaseURL: process.env.REACT_APP_PROD_DATABASE_URL,
  projectId: process.env.REACT_APP_PROD_PROJECT_ID,
  storageBucket: process.env.REACT_APP_PROD_STORAGE_BUCKET,
  messagingSenderId: process.env.REACT_APP_PROD_MESSAGING_SENDER_ID,
};

const devConfig = {
  apiKey: process.env.REACT_APP_DEV_API_KEY,
  authDomain: process.env.REACT_APP_DEV_AUTH_DOMAIN,
  databaseURL: process.env.REACT_APP_DEV_DATABASE_URL,
  projectId: process.env.REACT_APP_DEV_PROJECT_ID,
  storageBucket: process.env.REACT_APP_DEV_STORAGE_BUCKET,
  messagingSenderId: process.env.REACT_APP_DEV_MESSAGING_SENDER_ID,
};

const config =
  process.env.NODE_ENV === 'production' ? prodConfig : devConfig;

class Firebase {
  constructor() {
    app.initializeApp(config);
  }
```

```
}

export default Firebase;
```

An alternate way to implement this is to specify a dedicated *.env.development* and *.env.production* file for both kinds of environment variables in your project. Each file is used to define environmental variables for the matching environment. Defining a configuration becomes straightforward again, because you don't have to select the correct configuration yourself.

src/components/Firebase/firebase.js

```
import app from 'firebase/app';

const config = {
  apiKey: process.env.REACT_APP_API_KEY,
  authDomain: process.env.REACT_APP_AUTH_DOMAIN,
  databaseURL: process.env.REACT_APP_DATABASE_URL,
  projectId: process.env.REACT_APP_PROJECT_ID,
  storageBucket: process.env.REACT_APP_STORAGE_BUCKET,
  messagingSenderId: process.env.REACT_APP_MESSAGING_SENDER_ID,
};

class Firebase {
  constructor() {
    app.initializeApp(config);
  }
}

export default Firebase;
```

Whether you used environment variables, defined the configuration inline, used only one Firebase project, or multiple projects for each environment, you configured Firebase for your React application. The next section will show you how a Firebase instance created from the Firebase class is used in React.

Exercises:

- Read more about the Firebase Setup for Web Applications[33]
- Read more about Firebase's Pricing Plans[34] to know better about the limitations of the free plan.
- Confirm your source code for the last section[35]

---

[33]https://firebase.google.com/docs/web/setup
[34]https://firebase.google.com/pricing/
[35]http://bit.ly/2VqqWKP

Firebase in React

You created a Firebase class, but you are not using it in your React application yet. In this section, we'll connect the Firebase with the React world. The simple approach is to create a Firebase instance with the Firebase class, and then import the instance (or class) in every React component where it's needed. That's not the best approach though, for two reasons:

- It is more difficult to test your React components.
- It is more error prone, because Firebase should only be initialized once in your application (singleton[36]) and by exposing the Firebase class to every React component, you could end up by mistake with multiple Firebase instances.

An alternative way is to use React's Context API[37] to provide a Firebase instance once at the top-level of your component hierarchy. Create a new *src/components/Firebase/context.js* file in your Firebase module and provide the following implementation details:

src/components/Firebase/context.js

```
import React from 'react';

const FirebaseContext = React.createContext(null);

export default FirebaseContext;
```

The createContext() function essentially creates two components. The FirebaseContext.Provider component is used to provide a Firebase instance once at the top-level of your React component tree, which we will do in this section; and the FirebaseContext.Consumer component is used to retrieve the Firebase instance if it is needed in the React component. For a well-encapsulated Firebase module, we'll define a *index.js* file in our Firebase folder that exports all necessary functionalities (Firebase class, Firebase context for Consumer and Provider components):

---

[36]https://en.wikipedia.org/wiki/Singleton_pattern
[37]https://www.robinwieruch.de/react-context-api/

src/components/Firebase/index.js

```
import FirebaseContext from './context';
import Firebase from './firebase';

export default Firebase;

export { FirebaseContext };
```

The Firebase Context from the Firebase module (folder) is used to provide a Firebase instance to your entire application in the *src/index.js* file. You only need to create the Firebase instance with the Firebase class and pass it as value prop to the React's Context:

src/index.js

```
import React from 'react';
import ReactDOM from 'react-dom';

import './index.css';
import * as serviceWorker from './serviceWorker';

import App from './components/App';
import Firebase, { FirebaseContext } from './components/Firebase';

ReactDOM.render(
  <FirebaseContext.Provider value={new Firebase()}>
    <App />
  </FirebaseContext.Provider>,
  document.getElementById('root'),
);

serviceWorker.unregister();
```

Doing it this way, we can be assured that Firebase is only instantiated once and that it is injected via React's Context API to React's component tree. Now, every component that is interested in using Firebase has access to the Firebase instance with a `FirebaseContext.Consumer` component. Even though you will see it first-hand later for this application, the following code snippet shows how it would work:

Code Playground

```
import React from 'react';

import { FirebaseContext } from '../Firebase';

const SomeComponent = () => (
  <FirebaseContext.Consumer>
    {firebase => {
      return <div>I've access to Firebase and render something.</div>;
    }}
  </FirebaseContext.Consumer>
);

export default SomeComponent;
```

Firebase and React are now connected, the fundamental step to make the layers communicate with each other. Next, we will implement the interface for the Firebase class on our side to communicate with the Firebase API.

Exercises:

- Read more about React's Context API[38]
- Confirm your source code for the last section[39]

---

[38]https://www.robinwieruch.de/react-context-api/
[39]http://bit.ly/2VrUms0

Firebase's Authentication API

In the previous section, you created a Firebase project on the official Firebase website. This section will implement the interface of your Firebase class that enables communication between the class and the Firebase authentication API. In the sections afterward, you will use the interface of the Firebase class in your React components.

First, we need to activate one of the available authentication providers on Firebase's website. On your project's Firebase dashboard, you can find a menu item which says "Authentication". Select it and click "Sign-In Method" menu item afterward. There you can enable the authentication with Email/Password:

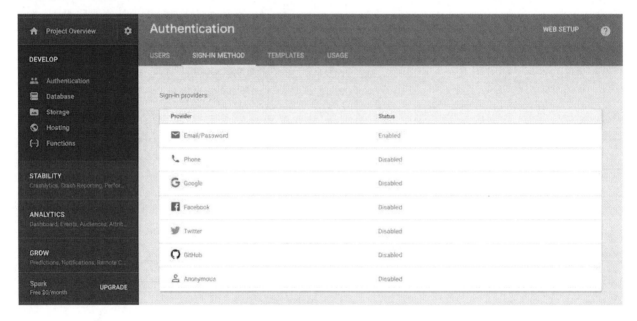

Second, we will implement the authentication API for our Firebase class. Import and instantiate the package from Firebase responsible for all the authentication in your *src/components/Firebase/firebase.js* file:

src/components/Firebase/firebase.js

```
import app from 'firebase/app';
import 'firebase/auth';

const config = {
  apiKey: process.env.REACT_APP_API_KEY,
  authDomain: process.env.REACT_APP_AUTH_DOMAIN,
  databaseURL: process.env.REACT_APP_DATABASE_URL,
  projectId: process.env.REACT_APP_PROJECT_ID,
  storageBucket: process.env.REACT_APP_STORAGE_BUCKET,
  messagingSenderId: process.env.REACT_APP_MESSAGING_SENDER_ID,
};

class Firebase {
  constructor() {
    app.initializeApp(config);

    this.auth = app.auth();
  }
}

export default Firebase;
```

Let's define all the authentication functions as class methods step by step. They will serve our communication channel from the Firebase class to the Firebase API. First, the sign up function (registration) takes email and password parameters for its function signature and uses an official Firebase API endpoint to create a user:

src/components/Firebase/firebase.js

```
import app from 'firebase/app';
import 'firebase/auth';

const config = { ... };

class Firebase {
  constructor() {
    app.initializeApp(config);

    this.auth = app.auth();
  }

  // *** Auth API ***
```

```
  doCreateUserWithEmailAndPassword = (email, password) =>
    this.auth.createUserWithEmailAndPassword(email, password);
}

export default Firebase;
```

We'll also set up the login/sign-in function, which takes email and password parameters, as well:

src/components/Firebase/firebase.js

```
import app from 'firebase/app';
import 'firebase/auth';

const config = { ... };

class Firebase {
  constructor() {
    app.initializeApp(config);

    this.auth = app.auth();
  }

  // *** Auth API ***

  doCreateUserWithEmailAndPassword = (email, password) =>
    this.auth.createUserWithEmailAndPassword(email, password);

  doSignInWithEmailAndPassword = (email, password) =>
    this.auth.signInWithEmailAndPassword(email, password);
}

export default Firebase;
```

These endpoints are called asynchronously, and they will need to be resolved later, as well as error handling. For instance, it is not possible to sign in a user who is not signed up yet since the Firebase API would return an error. In case of the sign out function, you don't need to pass any argument to it, because Firebase knows about the currently authenticated user. If no user is authenticated, nothing will happen when this function is called.

src/components/Firebase/firebase.js

```
import app from 'firebase/app';
import 'firebase/auth';

const config = { ... };

class Firebase {
  constructor() {
    app.initializeApp(config);

    this.auth = app.auth();
  }

  // *** Auth API ***

  doCreateUserWithEmailAndPassword = (email, password) =>
    this.auth.createUserWithEmailAndPassword(email, password);

  doSignInWithEmailAndPassword = (email, password) =>
    this.auth.signInWithEmailAndPassword(email, password);

  doSignOut = () => this.auth.signOut();
}

export default Firebase;
```

There are two more authentication methods to reset and change a password for an authenticated user:

src/components/Firebase/firebase.js

```
import app from 'firebase/app';
import 'firebase/auth';

const config = { ... };

class Firebase {
  constructor() {
    app.initializeApp(config);

    this.auth = app.auth();
  }
```

```
// *** Auth API ***

doCreateUserWithEmailAndPassword = (email, password) =>
  this.auth.createUserWithEmailAndPassword(email, password);

doSignInWithEmailAndPassword = (email, password) =>
  this.auth.signInWithEmailAndPassword(email, password);

doSignOut = () => this.auth.signOut();

doPasswordReset = email => this.auth.sendPasswordResetEmail(email);

doPasswordUpdate = password =>
  this.auth.currentUser.updatePassword(password);
}

export default Firebase;
```

That's the authentication interface for your React components that will connect to the Firebase API. In the next section, we will consume all the methods of your Firebase class in your React components.

Exercises:

- Read more about Firebase Authentication for Web[40]
- Confirm your source code for the last section[41]

---

[40]https://firebase.google.com/docs/auth/web/start
[41]http://bit.ly/2VpQ1pk

Sign Up with React and Firebase

We set up all the routes for your application, configured Firebase and implemented the authentication API for your Firebase class. It's also possible to use Firebase within your React components. Now it's time to use the authentication functionalities in your React components, which we'll build from scratch. I try to put most of the code in one block, because the components are not too small, and splitting them up step by step might be too verbose. Nevertheless, I will guide you through each code block afterward. The code blocks for forms can become repetitive, so they will be explained once well.

Let's start with the sign up page (registration page). It consists of the page, a form, and a link. The form is used to sign up a new user to your application with username, email, and password. The link will be used on the sign in page (login page) later if a user has no account yet. It is a redirect to the sign up page, but not used on the sign up page itself. Implement the *src/components/SignUp/index.js* file the following way:

src/components/SignUp/index.js

```
import React, { Component } from 'react';
import { Link } from 'react-router-dom';

import * as ROUTES from '../../constants/routes';

const SignUpPage = () => (
  <div>
    <h1>SignUp</h1>
    <SignUpForm />
  </div>
);

class SignUpForm extends Component {
  constructor(props) {
    super(props);
  }

  onSubmit = event => {

  }

  onChange = event => {

  };

  render() {
```

```
    return (
      <form onSubmit={this.onSubmit}>

      </form>
    );
  }
}

const SignUpLink = () => (
  <p>
    Don't have an account? <Link to={ROUTES.SIGN_UP}>Sign Up</Link>
  </p>
);

export default SignUpPage;

export { SignUpForm, SignUpLink };
```

The SignUpForm component is the only React class component in this file, because it has to manage the form state in React's local state. There are two pieces missing in the current SignUpForm component: the form content in the render method in terms of input fields to capture the information (email address, password, etc.) of a user and the implementation of the onSubmit class method when a user signs up eventually.

First, let's initialize the state of the component. It will capture the user information such as username, email, and password. There will be a second password field/state for a password confirmation. In addition, there is an error state to capture an error object in case of the sign up request to the Firebase API fails. The state is initialized by an object destructuring. This way, we can use the initial state object to reset the state after a successful sign up.

src/components/SignUp/index.js

```
...

const INITIAL_STATE = {
  username: '',
  email: '',
  passwordOne: '',
  passwordTwo: '',
  error: null,
};

class SignUpForm extends Component {
  constructor(props) {
```

```
  super(props);

  this.state = { ...INITIAL_STATE };
  }

  ...

}

...
```

Let's implement all the input fields to capture the information in the render method of the component. The input fields need to update the local state of the component by using a onChange handler.

src/components/SignUp/index.js

```
...

class SignUpForm extends Component {

  ...

  onChange = event => {
    this.setState({ [event.target.name]: event.target.value });
  };

  render() {
    const {
      username,
      email,
      passwordOne,
      passwordTwo,
      error,
    } = this.state;

    return (
      <form onSubmit={this.onSubmit}>
        <input
          name="username"
          value={username}
          onChange={this.onChange}
          type="text"
          placeholder="Full Name"
```

```
      />
      <input
        name="email"
        value={email}
        onChange={this.onChange}
        type="text"
        placeholder="Email Address"
      />
      <input
        name="passwordOne"
        value={passwordOne}
        onChange={this.onChange}
        type="password"
        placeholder="Password"
      />
      <input
        name="passwordTwo"
        value={passwordTwo}
        onChange={this.onChange}
        type="password"
        placeholder="Confirm Password"
      />
      <button type="submit">Sign Up</button>

      {error && <p>{error.message}</p>}
    </form>
  );
 }
}
```

. . .

Let's take the last implemented code block apart. All the input fields implement the unidirectional data flow of React; thus, each input field gets a value from the local state and updates the value in the local state with a onChange handler. The input fields are controlled by the local state of the component and don't control their own states. They are controlled components.

In the last part of the form, there is an optional error message from an error object. The error objects from Firebase have this message property by default, so you can rely on it to display the proper text for your application's user. However, the message is only shown when there is an actual error using a conditional rendering[42].

---

[42]https://www.robinwieruch.de/conditional-rendering-react/

One piece in the form is missing: validation. Let's use an isInvalid boolean to enable or disable the submit button.

src/components/SignUp/index.js

```
...

class SignUpForm extends Component {

  ...

  render() {
    const {
      username,
      email,
      passwordOne,
      passwordTwo,
      error,
    } = this.state;

    const isInvalid =
      passwordOne !== passwordTwo ||
      passwordOne === '' ||
      email === '' ||
      username === '';

    return (
      <form onSubmit={this.onSubmit}>
        <input
          ...
        <button disabled={isInvalid} type="submit">
          Sign Up
        </button>

        {error && <p>{error.message}</p>}
      </form>
    );
  }
}

...
```

The user is only allowed to sign up if both passwords are the same, and if the username, email and at least one password are filled with a string. This is password confirmation in a common sign up process.

You should be able to visit the */signup* route in your browser after starting your application to confirm that the form with all its input fields shows up. You should also be able to type into it (confirmation that the local state updates are working) and able to enable the submit button by providing all input fields a string (confirmation that the validation works).

What's missing in the component is the onSubmit() class method, which will pass all the form data to the Firebase authentication API via your authentication interface in the Firebase class:

src/components/SignUp/index.js

```
. . .

class SignUpForm extends Component {

  . . .

  onSubmit = event => {
    const { username, email, passwordOne } = this.state;

    this.props.firebase
      .doCreateUserWithEmailAndPassword(email, passwordOne)
      .then(authUser => {
        this.setState({ ...INITIAL_STATE });
      })
      .catch(error => {
        this.setState({ error });
      });

    event.preventDefault();
  };

  . . .

}

. . .
```

The code is not working yet, but let's break down what we have so far. All the necessary information passed to the authentication API can be destructured from the local state. You will only need one password property, because both password strings should be the same after the validation.

Next, call the sign up function defined in the previous section in the Firebase class, which takes the email and the password property. The username is not used yet for the sign up process, but will be used later.

If the request resolves successfully, you can set the local state of the component to its initial state to empty the input fields. If the request is rejected, you will run into the catch block and set the error object in the local state. An error message should show up in the form due to the conditional rendering in your component's render method.

Also, the `preventDefault()` method on the event prevents a reload of the browser which otherwise would be a natural behavior when using a submit in a form. Note that the signed up user object from the Firebase API is available in the callback function of the then block in our request. You will use it later with the username.

You may have also noticed that one essential piece is missing: We didn't make the Firebase instance available in the SignUpForm component's props[43] yet. Let's change this by utilizing our Firebase Context in the SignUpPage component, and by passing the Firebase instance to the SignUpForm.

src/components/SignUp/index.js

```
import React, { Component } from 'react';
import { Link } from 'react-router-dom';

import { FirebaseContext } from '../Firebase';
import * as ROUTES from '../../constants/routes';

const SignUpPage = () => (
  <div>
    <h1>SignUp</h1>
    <FirebaseContext.Consumer>
      {firebase => <SignUpForm firebase={firebase} />}
    </FirebaseContext.Consumer>
  </div>
);

const INITIAL_STATE = { ... };

class SignUpForm extends Component {
  ...
}

...
```

Now the registration of a new user should work. However, I'd like to make one improvement on how we access the Firebase instance here. Rather than using a render prop component[44], which is automatically given with React's Context Consumer component, it may be simpler to use a higher-order component[45]. Let's implement this higher-order component:

[43]https://www.robinwieruch.de/react-pass-props-to-component/
[44]https://www.robinwieruch.de/react-render-props-pattern/
[45]https://www.robinwieruch.de/gentle-introduction-higher-order-components/

src/components/Firebase/context.js

```
import React from 'react';

const FirebaseContext = React.createContext(null);

export const withFirebase = Component => props => (
  <FirebaseContext.Consumer>
    {firebase => <Component {...props} firebase={firebase} />}
  </FirebaseContext.Consumer>
);

export default FirebaseContext;
```

Next, make it available via our Firebase module in the *src/components/Firebase/index.js* file:

src/components/Firebase/index.js

```
import FirebaseContext, { withFirebase } from './context';
import Firebase from './firebase';

export default Firebase;

export { FirebaseContext, withFirebase };
```

Now, instead of using the Firebase Context directly in the SignUpPage, which doesn't need to know about the Firebase instance, use the higher-order component to wrap your SignUpForm. Afterward, the SignUpForm has access to the Firebase instance via the higher-order component. It's also possible to use the SignUpForm as standalone without the SignUpPage, because it is responsible to get the Firebase instance via the higher-order component.

src/components/SignUp/index.js

```
import React, { Component } from 'react';
import { Link } from 'react-router-dom';

import { withFirebase } from '../Firebase';
import * as ROUTES from '../../constants/routes';

const SignUpPage = () => (
  <div>
    <h1>SignUp</h1>
    <SignUpForm />
  </div>
```

```
);

const INITIAL_STATE = { ... };

class SignUpFormBase extends Component {
  ...
}

const SignUpLink = () => ...

const SignUpForm = withFirebase(SignUpFormBase);

export default SignUpPage;

export { SignUpForm, SignUpLink };
```

When a user signs up to your application, you want to redirect the user to another page. It could be the user's home page, a protected route for only authenticated users. You will need the help of React Router to redirect the user after a successful sign up.

src/components/SignUp/index.js

```
import React, { Component } from 'react';
import { Link, withRouter } from 'react-router-dom';

import { withFirebase } from '../Firebase';
import * as ROUTES from '../../constants/routes';

...

class SignUpFormBase extends Component {

  ...

  onSubmit = (event) => {
    const { username, email, passwordOne } = this.state;

    this.props.firebase
      .doCreateUserWithEmailAndPassword(email, passwordOne)
      .then(authUser => {
        this.setState({ ...INITIAL_STATE });
        this.props.history.push(ROUTES.HOME);
      })
```

```
      .catch(error => {
        this.setState({ error });
      });

    event.preventDefault();
  }


  ...
}


...


const SignUpForm = withRouter(withFirebase(SignUpFormBase));

export default SignUpPage;

export { SignUpForm, SignUpLink };
```

Let's take the previous code block apart again. To redirect a user to another page programmatically, we need access to React Router to redirect the user to another page. Fortunately, the React Router node package offers a higher-order component to make the router properties accessible in the props of a component. Any component that goes in the withRouter() higher-order component gains access to all the properties of the router, so when passing the enhanced SignUpFormBase component to the withRouter() higher-order component, it has access to the props of the router. The relevant property from the router props is the history object, because it allows us to redirect a user to another page by pushing a route to it.

The history object of the router can be used in the onSubmit() class method eventually. If a request resolves successfully, you can push any route to the history object. Since the pushed */home* route is defined in our App component with a matching component to be rendered, the displayed page component will change after the redirect.

There is one improvement that we can make for the higher-order components used for the SignUpForm. Nesting functions (higher-order components) into each other like we did before can become verbose. A better way is to compose the higher-order components instead. To do this, install recompose[46] for your application on the command line:

Command Line

```
npm install recompose
```

You can use recompose to organize your higher-order components. Since the higher-order components don't depend on each other, the order doesn't matter. Otherwise, it may be good to know that the compose function applies the higher-order components from right to left.

---

[46]https://github.com/acdlite/recompose

src/components/SignUp/index.js

```
import React, { Component } from 'react';
import { Link, withRouter } from 'react-router-dom';
import { compose } from 'recompose';

import { withFirebase } from '../Firebase';
import * as ROUTES from '../../constants/routes';

...

const SignUpForm = compose(
  withRouter,
  withFirebase,
)(SignUpFormBase);

export default SignUpPage;

export { SignUpForm, SignUpLink };
```

Run your application again. If you signed up a user successfully, it should redirect to the home page. If the sign up fails, you should see an error message. Try to sign up a user with the same email address twice and verify that a similar error message shows up: "The email address is already in use by another account.". Congratulations, you signed up your first user via Firebase authentication.

Exercises:

- Read more about data fetching in React[47]
- Read more about higher-order components in React[48]
- Read more about render prop components in React[49]
- Confirm your source code for the last section[50]

---

[47]https://www.robinwieruch.de/react-fetching-data/
[48]https://www.robinwieruch.de/gentle-introduction-higher-order-components/
[49]https://www.robinwieruch.de/react-render-props-pattern/
[50]http://bit.ly/2VkrTEA

Sign In with React and Firebase

A sign up automatically results in a sign in/login by the user. We cannot rely on this mechanic, however, since a user could be signed up but not signed in. Let's implement the login with Firebase now. It is similar to the sign up mechanism and components, so this time we won't split it into so many code blocks:

src/components/SignIn/index.js

```
import React, { Component } from 'react';
import { withRouter } from 'react-router-dom';
import { compose } from 'recompose';

import { SignUpLink } from '../SignUp';
import { withFirebase } from '../Firebase';
import * as ROUTES from '../../constants/routes';

const SignInPage = () => (
  <div>
    <h1>SignIn</h1>
    <SignInForm />
    <SignUpLink />
  </div>
);

const INITIAL_STATE = {
  email: '',
  password: '',
  error: null,
};

class SignInFormBase extends Component {
  constructor(props) {
    super(props);

    this.state = { ...INITIAL_STATE };
  }

  onSubmit = event => {
    const { email, password } = this.state;

    this.props.firebase
      .doSignInWithEmailAndPassword(email, password)
```

```jsx
      .then(() => {
        this.setState({ ...INITIAL_STATE });
        this.props.history.push(ROUTES.HOME);
      })
      .catch(error => {
        this.setState({ error });
      });

    event.preventDefault();
  };

  onChange = event => {
    this.setState({ [event.target.name]: event.target.value });
  };

  render() {
    const { email, password, error } = this.state;

    const isInvalid = password === '' || email === '';

    return (
      <form onSubmit={this.onSubmit}>
        <input
          name="email"
          value={email}
          onChange={this.onChange}
          type="text"
          placeholder="Email Address"
        />
        <input
          name="password"
          value={password}
          onChange={this.onChange}
          type="password"
          placeholder="Password"
        />
        <button disabled={isInvalid} type="submit">
          Sign In
        </button>

        {error && <p>{error.message}</p>}
      </form>
    );
```

```
  }
}

const SignInForm = compose(
  withRouter,
  withFirebase,
)(SignInFormBase);

export default SignInPage;

export { SignInForm };
```

It is almost the same as the sign up form. Its input fields capture all the necessary information like username and password. A validation step makes sure the email and password are set before performing the request by enabling or disabling the submit button. The authentication API is used again, this time with a function to sign in the user rather than sign them up. If sign in succeeds, the local state is updated with the initial state and the user is redirected again. If the sign in fails, an error object is stored in the local state and an error message appears. The SignUpLink, which was defined earlier in the SignUp module, is used on the sign in page. It lets users sign up if they don't have an account, and it is found on the sign in page.

Exercises:

- Familiarize yourself with the SignIn and SignInForm components.
  - If they are mysterious to you, checkout the previous section with the implementation of the SignUpForm again
- Confirm your source code for the last section[51]

---

[51]http://bit.ly/2VnEzup

Sign Out with React and Firebase

To complete the authentication loop, next we'll implement the sign out component. The component is just a button that appears within the Navigation component. Since we can use the previously-defined authentication API to sign out a user, passing functionality to a button in a React component is fairly straightforward.

src/components/SignOut/index.js

```
import React from 'react';

import { withFirebase } from '../Firebase';

const SignOutButton = ({ firebase }) => (
  <button type="button" onClick={firebase.doSignOut}>
    Sign Out
  </button>
);

export default withFirebase(SignOutButton);
```

The SignOutButton has access to the Firebase instance using the higher-order component again. Now, use the SignOutButton in the Navigation component:

src/components/Navigation/index.js

```
import React from 'react';
import { Link } from 'react-router-dom';

import SignOutButton from '../SignOut';
import * as ROUTES from '../../constants/routes';

const Navigation = () => (
  <div>
    <ul>
      <li>
        <Link to={ROUTES.SIGN_IN}>Sign In</Link>
      </li>
      <li>
        <Link to={ROUTES.LANDING}>Landing</Link>
      </li>
      <li>
        <Link to={ROUTES.HOME}>Home</Link>
      </li>
```

```
    <li>
      <Link to={ROUTES.ACCOUNT}>Account</Link>
    </li>
    <li>
      <Link to={ROUTES.ADMIN}>Admin</Link>
    </li>
    <li>
      <SignOutButton />
    </li>
    </ul>
  </div>
);


export default Navigation;
```

Regarding components, everything is set to fulfil a full authentication roundtrip. Users can sign up (register), sign in (login), and sign out (logout).

Exercises:

- Read more about Firebase Authentication with E-Mail/Password[52]
- Confirm your source code for the last section[53]

---

[52]https://firebase.google.com/docs/auth/web/password-auth
[53]http://bit.ly/2VpQ9oO

Session Handling

This section is the most important one for the authentication process. You have all the components needed to fulfil an authentication roundtrip in React, and all that's missing is an overseer for the session state. Logic regarding the current authenticated user needs to be stored and made accessible to other components. This is often the point where developers start to use a state management library like Redux or MobX[54]. Without these, we'll make due using global state[55] instead of state management libraries.

Since our application is made under the umbrella of App component, it's sufficient to manage the session state in the App component using React's local state. The App component only needs to keep track of an authenticated user (session). If a user is authenticated, store it in the local state and pass the authenticated user object down to all components that are interested in it. Otherwise, pass the authenticated user down as null. That way, all components interested in it can adjust their behavior (e.g. use conditional rendering) based on the session state. For instance, the Navigation component is interested because it has to show different options to authenticated and non authenticated users. The SignOut component shouldn't show up for a non authenticated user, for example.

We handle session handling in the App component in the *src/components/App/index.js* file. Because the component handles local state now, you have to refactor it to a class component. It manages the local state of a authUser object, and then passes it to the Navigation component.

src/components/App/index.js

```
import React, { Component } from 'react';
import { BrowserRouter as Router, Route } from 'react-router-dom';

...

class App extends Component {
  constructor(props) {
    super(props);

    this.state = {
      authUser: null,
    };
  }

  render() {
    return (
      <Router>
        <div>
          <Navigation authUser={this.state.authUser} />
```

---

[54]https://www.robinwieruch.de/redux-mobx-confusion/
[55]https://www.robinwieruch.de/react-global-state-without-redux/

```
        <hr/>

        ...
      </div>
    </Router>
  );
  }
}


export default App;
```

The Navigation component can be made aware of authenticated user to display different options. It should either show the available links for an authenticated user or a non authenticated user.

src/components/Navigation/index.js

```
import React from 'react';
import { Link } from 'react-router-dom';

import SignOutButton from '../SignOut';
import * as ROUTES from '../../constants/routes';

const Navigation = ({ authUser }) => (
  <div>{authUser ? <NavigationAuth /> : <NavigationNonAuth />}</div>
);


const NavigationAuth = () => (
  <ul>
    <li>
      <Link to={ROUTES.LANDING}>Landing</Link>
    </li>
    <li>
      <Link to={ROUTES.HOME}>Home</Link>
    </li>
    <li>
      <Link to={ROUTES.ACCOUNT}>Account</Link>
    </li>
    <li>
      <SignOutButton />
    </li>
  </ul>
);
```

```
const NavigationNonAuth = () => (
  <ul>
    <li>
      <Link to={ROUTES.LANDING}>Landing</Link>
    </li>
    <li>
      <Link to={ROUTES.SIGN_IN}>Sign In</Link>
    </li>
  </ul>
);


export default Navigation;
```

Let's see where the authUser (authenticated user) comes from in the App component. Firebase offers a listener function to get the authenticated user from Firebase:

src/components/App/index.js

```
. . .

import * as ROUTES from '../constants/routes';
import { withFirebase } from '../Firebase';

class App extends Component {
  constructor(props) {
    super(props);

    this.state = {
      authUser: null,
    };
  }

  componentDidMount() {
    this.props.firebase.auth.onAuthStateChanged(authUser => {
      authUser
        ? this.setState({ authUser })
        : this.setState({ authUser: null });
    });
  }


  . . .


}
```

```
export default withFirebase(App);
```

The helper function onAuthStateChanged() receives a function as parameter that has access to the authenticated user. Also, the passed function is called every time something changes for the authenticated user. It is called when a user signs up, signs in, and signs out. If a user signs out, the authUser object becomes null, so the authUser property in the local state is set to null and all components depending on it adjust their behavior (e.g. display different options like the Navigation component).

We also want to avoid memory leaks that lead to performance issues[56], so we'll remove the listener if the component unmounts.

src/components/App/index.js

```
...

class App extends Component {
  ...

  componentDidMount() {
    this.listener = this.props.firebase.auth.onAuthStateChanged(
      authUser => {
        authUser
          ? this.setState({ authUser })
          : this.setState({ authUser: null });
      },
    );
  }

  componentWillUnmount() {
    this.listener();
  }

  ...

}

export default withFirebase(App);
```

Start your application and verify that your sign up, sign in, and sign out functionality works, and that the Navigation component displays the options depending on the session state (authenticated user).

---

[56]https://www.robinwieruch.de/react-warning-cant-call-setstate-on-an-unmounted-component/

Congratulations, you have successfully implemented the authentication process with Firebase in React. Everything in the following sections reagrding authentication is considered extra, to improve the developer's experience and add a couple of useful features along the way.

Exercises:

- Read more about Firebase's Authenticated User[57]
- Confirm your source code for the last section[58]

---

[57]https://firebase.google.com/docs/auth/web/manage-users
[58]http://bit.ly/2VrULL2

Session Handling with Higher-Order Components

We added a basic version of session handling in the last section. However, the authenticated user still needs to be passed down from the App component to interested parties. That can become tedious over time, because the authenticated user has to be passed through all components until it reaches all the leaf components. You used the React Context API to pass down the Firebase instance to any component before. Here, you will do the same for the authenticated user. In a new *src/components/Session/context.js* file, place the following new React Context for the session (authenticated user):

src/components/Session/context.js

```
import React from 'react';

const AuthUserContext = React.createContext(null);

export default AuthUserContext;
```

Next, import and export it from the *src/components/Session/index.js* file that is the entry point to this module:

src/components/Session/index.js

```
import AuthUserContext from './context';

export { AuthUserContext };
```

The App component can use the new context to provide the authenticated user to components that are interested in it:

src/components/App/index.js

```
...

import { AuthUserContext } from '../Session';

class App extends Component {
  ...

  render() {
    return (
      <AuthUserContext.Provider value={this.state.authUser}>
        <Router>
          <div>
```

```
        <Navigation />

        <hr />

          ...

      </div>
    </Router>
  </AuthUserContext.Provider>
    );
  }
}


export default withFirebase(App);
```

The `authUser` doesn't need to be passed to the Navigation component anymore. Instead, the Navigation component uses the new context to consume the authenticated user:

src/components/Navigation/index.js

```
...

import { AuthUserContext } from '../Session';

const Navigation = () => (
  <div>
    <AuthUserContext.Consumer>
      {authUser =>
        authUser ? <NavigationAuth /> : <NavigationNonAuth />
      }
    </AuthUserContext.Consumer>
  </div>
);
```

The application works the same as before, except any component can simply use React's Context to consume the authenticated user. To keep the App component clean and concise, I like to extract the session handling for the authenticated user to a separate higher-order component in a new *src/components/Session/withAuthentication.js* file:

src/components/Session/withAuthentication.js

```
import React from 'react';

const withAuthentication = Component => {
  class WithAuthentication extends React.Component {
    render() {
      return <Component {...this.props} />;
    }
  }

  return WithAuthentication;
};


export default withAuthentication;
```

Move all logic that deals with the authenticated user from the App component to it:

src/components/Session/withAuthentication.js

```
import React from 'react';

import AuthUserContext from './context';
import { withFirebase } from '../Firebase';

const withAuthentication = Component => {
  class WithAuthentication extends React.Component {
    constructor(props) {
      super(props);

      this.state = {
        authUser: null,
      };
    }

    componentDidMount() {
      this.listener = this.props.firebase.auth.onAuthStateChanged(
        authUser => {
          authUser
            ? this.setState({ authUser })
            : this.setState({ authUser: null });
        },
      );
    }
```

```
  componentWillUnmount() {
    this.listener();
  }

  render() {
    return (
      <AuthUserContext.Provider value={this.state.authUser}>
        <Component {...this.props} />
      </AuthUserContext.Provider>
    );
  }
}

  return withFirebase(WithAuthentication);
};


export default withAuthentication;
```

As you can see, it also uses the new React Context to provide the authenticated user. The App component will not be in charge of it anymore. Next, export the higher-order component from the *src/components/Session/index.js* file, so that it can be used in the App component after:

src/components/Session/index.js

```
import AuthUserContext from './context';
import withAuthentication from './withAuthentication';


export { AuthUserContext, withAuthentication };
```

The App component becomes a function component again, without the additional business logic for the authenticated user. Now, it uses the higher-order component to make the authenticated user available for all other components below of the App component:

src/components/App/index.js

```
import React from 'react';
import { BrowserRouter as Router, Route } from 'react-router-dom';

import Navigation from '../Navigation';
import LandingPage from '../Landing';
import SignUpPage from '../SignUp';
import SignInPage from '../SignIn';
import PasswordForgetPage from '../PasswordForget';
import HomePage from '../Home';
import AccountPage from '../Account';
import AdminPage from '../Admin';

import * as ROUTES from '../../constants/routes';
import { withAuthentication } from '../Session';

const App = () => (
  <Router>
    <div>
      <Navigation />

      <hr />

      <Route exact path={ROUTES.LANDING} component={LandingPage} />
      <Route path={ROUTES.SIGN_UP} component={SignUpPage} />
      <Route path={ROUTES.SIGN_IN} component={SignInPage} />
      <Route
        path={ROUTES.PASSWORD_FORGET}
        component={PasswordForgetPage}
      />
      <Route path={ROUTES.HOME} component={HomePage} />
      <Route path={ROUTES.ACCOUNT} component={AccountPage} />
      <Route path={ROUTES.ADMIN} component={AdminPage} />
    </div>
  </Router>
);

export default withAuthentication(App);
```

Start the application and verify that it still works. You didn't change any behavior in this section, but shielded away the more complex logic into a higher-order component. Also, the application now passes the authenticated user implicitly via React's Context, rather than explicitly through the component tree using props.

Exercises:

- Check again your Firebase Context and higher-order component implementation in the *src/components/Firebase* module, which is quite similar to what you have done in this section.
- Confirm your source code for the last section[59]

---

[59]http://bit.ly/2VjYz0R

Password Management

Let's take a step back from the higher-order components, React Context API, and session handling. In this section, we will implement two additional features available in the Firebase authentication API, the ability to retrieve (password forget) and change a password.

Password Forget

Let's start by implementing the password forget feature. Since you already implemented the interface in your Firebase class, you can use it in components. The following file adds most of the password reset logic in a form again. We already used a couple of those forms before, so it shouldn't be different now. Add this in the *src/components/PasswordForget/index.js* file:

src/components/PasswordForget/index.js

```
import React, { Component } from 'react';
import { Link } from 'react-router-dom';

import { withFirebase } from '../Firebase';
import * as ROUTES from '../../constants/routes';

const PasswordForgetPage = () => (
  <div>
    <h1>PasswordForget</h1>
    <PasswordForgetForm />
  </div>
);

const INITIAL_STATE = {
  email: '',
  error: null,
};

class PasswordForgetFormBase extends Component {
  constructor(props) {
    super(props);

    this.state = { ...INITIAL_STATE };
  }

  onSubmit = event => {
    const { email } = this.state;

    this.props.firebase
      .doPasswordReset(email)
      .then(() => {
        this.setState({ ...INITIAL_STATE });
      })
      .catch(error => {
```

```
        this.setState({ error });
      });

    event.preventDefault();
  };

  onChange = event => {
    this.setState({ [event.target.name]: event.target.value });
  };

  render() {
    const { email, error } = this.state;

    const isInvalid = email === '';

    return (
      <form onSubmit={this.onSubmit}>
        <input
          name="email"
          value={this.state.email}
          onChange={this.onChange}
          type="text"
          placeholder="Email Address"
        />
        <button disabled={isInvalid} type="submit">
          Reset My Password
        </button>

        {error && <p>{error.message}</p>}
      </form>
    );
  }
}

const PasswordForgetLink = () => (
  <p>
    <Link to={ROUTES.PASSWORD_FORGET}>Forgot Password?</Link>
  </p>
);

export default PasswordForgetPage;

const PasswordForgetForm = withFirebase(PasswordForgetFormBase);
```

```
export { PasswordForgetForm, PasswordForgetLink };
```

The code is verbose, but it it's no different from the sign up and sign in forms from previous sections. The password forget uses a form to submit the information (email address) needed by the Firebase authentication API to reset the password. A class method (onSubmit) ensures the information is send to the API. It also resets the form's input field on a successful request, and shows an error on an erroneous request. The form is validated before it is submitted as well. The file implements a password forget link as a component which isn't used directly in the form component. It is similar to the SignUpLink component that we used on in the SignInPage component. This link is the same, and it's still usable. If a user forgets the password after sign up, the password forget page uses the link in the *src/components/SignIn/index.js* file:

src/components/SignIn/index.js

```
import React, { Component } from 'react';
import { withRouter } from 'react-router-dom';
import { compose } from 'recompose';

import { SignUpLink } from '../SignUp';
import { PasswordForgetLink } from '../PasswordForget';
import { withFirebase } from '../Firebase';
import * as ROUTES from '../../constants/routes';

const SignInPage = () => (
  <div>
    <h1>SignIn</h1>
    <SignInForm />
    <PasswordForgetLink />
    <SignUpLink />
  </div>
);
```

. . .

The password forget page is already matched in the App component, so you can drop the PasswordForgetLink component in the sign in page and know the mapping between route and component is complete. Start the application and reset your password. It doesn't matter if you are authenticated or not. Once you send the request, you should get an email from Firebase to update your password.

Password Change

Next we'll add the password change feature, which is also in your Firebase interface. You only need a form component to use it. Again, the form component isn't any different from the sign in, sign up, and password forget forms. In the *src/components/PasswordChange/index.js* file add the following component:

src/components/PasswordChange/index.js

```
import React, { Component } from 'react';

import { withFirebase } from '../Firebase';

const INITIAL_STATE = {
  passwordOne: '',
  passwordTwo: '',
  error: null,
};

class PasswordChangeForm extends Component {
  constructor(props) {
    super(props);

    this.state = { ...INITIAL_STATE };
  }

  onSubmit = event => {
    const { passwordOne } = this.state;

    this.props.firebase
      .doPasswordUpdate(passwordOne)
      .then(() => {
        this.setState({ ...INITIAL_STATE });
      })
      .catch(error => {
        this.setState({ error });
      });

    event.preventDefault();
  };

  onChange = event => {
    this.setState({ [event.target.name]: event.target.value });
```

```
  };

  render() {
    const { passwordOne, passwordTwo, error } = this.state;

    const isInvalid =
      passwordOne !== passwordTwo || passwordOne === '';

    return (
      <form onSubmit={this.onSubmit}>
        <input
          name="passwordOne"
          value={passwordOne}
          onChange={this.onChange}
          type="password"
          placeholder="New Password"
        />
        <input
          name="passwordTwo"
          value={passwordTwo}
          onChange={this.onChange}
          type="password"
          placeholder="Confirm New Password"
        />
        <button disabled={isInvalid} type="submit">
          Reset My Password
        </button>

        {error && <p>{error.message}</p>}
      </form>
    );
  }
}

export default withFirebase(PasswordChangeForm);
```

The component updates its local state using onChange handlers in the input fields. It validates the state before submitting a request to change the password by enabling or disabling the submit button, and it shows again an error message when a request fails.

So far, the PasswordChangeForm is not matched by any route, because it should live on the Account page. The Account page could serve as the central place for users to manage their account, where it shows the PasswordChangeForm and PasswordResetForm, accessible by a standalone route.

You already created the *src/components/Account/index.js* file and matched the route in the App component. You only need to implement it:

src/components/Account/index.js

```
import React from 'react';

import { PasswordForgetForm } from '../PasswordForget';
import PasswordChangeForm from '../PasswordChange';

const AccountPage = () => (
  <div>
    <h1>Account Page</h1>
    <PasswordForgetForm />
    <PasswordChangeForm />
  </div>
);

export default AccountPage;
```

The Account page doesn't have any business logic. It uses the password forget and password change forms in a central place. In this section, your user experience improved significantly with the password forget and password change features, handling scenarios where users have trouble remembering passwords.

Exercises:

- Consider ways to protect the Account page and make it accessible only for authenticated users.
- Confirm your source code for the last section[60]

---

[60]http://bit.ly/2VqWgt4

Authorization (1): General Authorization and Route Protection

So far, all of your application's routes are accessible by everyone. It doesn't matter whether the user is authenticated or not authenticated. For instance, when you sign out on the home or account page, there is no redirect, even though these pages should be only accessible for authenticated users. There is no reason to show a non authenticated user the account or home page in the first place, because these are the places where a user accesses sensible information. In this section, so you will implement a protection for these routes called authorization. The protection is a **broad-grained authorization**, which checks for authenticated users. If none is present, it redirects from a protected to a public route; else, it will do nothing. The condition is defined as:

Code Playground

```
const condition = authUser => authUser != null;

// short version
const condition = authUser => !!authUser;
```

In contrast, a more **fine-grained authorization** could be a role-based or permission-based authorization:

Code Playground

```
// role-based authorization
const condition = authUser => authUser.role === 'ADMIN';

// permission-based authorization
const condition = authUser => authUser.permissions.canEditAccount;
```

Fortunately, we implement it in a way that lets you define the authorization condition (predicate) with flexibility, so that you can use a more generalized authorization rule, permission-based or role-based authorizations.

Like the withAuthentication higher-order component, there is a withAuthorization higher-order component to shield the authorization business logic from your components. It can be used on any component that needs to be protected with authorization (e.g. home page, account page). Let's start to add the higher-order component in a new file:

src/components/Session/withAuthorization.js

```
import React from 'react';

const withAuthorization = () => Component => {
  class WithAuthorization extends React.Component {
    render() {
      return <Component {...this.props} />;
    }
  }

  return WithAuthorization;
};

export default withAuthorization;
```

So far, the higher-order component is not doing anything but taking a component as input and returning it as output. However, the higher-order component should be able to receive a condition function passed as parameter. You can decide if it should be a broad or fine-grained (role-based, permission-based) authorization rule. Second, it has to decide based on the condition whether it should redirect to a public page (public route), because the user isn't authorized to view the current protected page (protected route). Let's paste the implementation details for the higher-order component and go through it step-by-step:

src/components/Session/withAuthorization.js

```
import React from 'react';
import { withRouter } from 'react-router-dom';
import { compose } from 'recompose';

import { withFirebase } from '../Firebase';
import * as ROUTES from '../../constants/routes';

const withAuthorization = condition => Component => {
  class WithAuthorization extends React.Component {
    componentDidMount() {
      this.listener = this.props.firebase.auth.onAuthStateChanged(
        authUser => {
          if (!condition(authUser)) {
            this.props.history.push(ROUTES.SIGN_IN);
          }
        },
      );
    }
```

```
    componentWillUnmount() {
      this.listener();
    }

    render() {
      return (
        <Component {...this.props} />
      );
    }
  }

  return compose(
    withRouter,
    withFirebase,
  )(WithAuthorization);
};

export default withAuthorization;
```

The render method displays the passed component (e.g. home page, account page) that should be protected by this higher-order component. We will refine this later. The real authorization logic happens in the componentDidMount() lifecycle method. Like the withAuthentication() higher-order component, it uses the Firebase listener to trigger a callback function every time the authenticated user changes. The authenticated user is either a authUser object or null. Within this function, the passed condition() function is executed with the authUser. If the authorization fails, for instance because the authenticated user is null, the higher-order component redirects to the sign in page. If it doesn't fail, the higher-order component does nothing and renders the passed component (e.g. home page, account page). To redirect a user, the higher-order component has access to the history object of the Router using the in-house withRouter() higher-order component from the React Router library.

Remember to export the higher-order component from your session module:

src/components/Session/index.js

```
import AuthUserContext from './context';
import withAuthentication from './withAuthentication';
import withAuthorization from './withAuthorization';


export { AuthUserContext, withAuthentication, withAuthorization };
```

In the next step, you can use the higher-order component to protect your routes (e.g. /home and /account) with authorization rules using the passed condition() function. To keep it simple, the following two components are only protected with a broad authorization rule that checks if the authUser is not null. First, enhance the HomePage component with the higher-order component and define the authorization condition for it:

src/components/Home/index.js

```
import React from 'react';

import { withAuthorization } from '../Session';

const HomePage = () => (
  <div>
    <h1>Home Page</h1>
    <p>The Home Page is accessible by every signed in user.</p>
  </div>
);

const condition = authUser => !!authUser;

export default withAuthorization(condition)(HomePage);
```

Second, enhance the AccountPage component with the higher-order component and define the authorization condition. It similar to the previous usage:

src/components/Account/index.js

```
import React from 'react';

import { PasswordForgetForm } from '../PasswordForget';
import PasswordChangeForm from '../PasswordChange';
import { withAuthorization } from '../Session';

const AccountPage = () => (
  <div>
    <h1>Account Page</h1>
    <PasswordForgetForm />
    <PasswordChangeForm />
  </div>
);

const condition = authUser => !!authUser;

export default withAuthorization(condition)(AccountPage);
```

The protection of both pages/routes is almost done. One refinement can be made in the `withAuthorization` higher-order component using the authenticated user from the context:

src/components/Session/withAuthorization.js

```
import React from 'react';
import { withRouter } from 'react-router-dom';
import { compose } from 'recompose';

import AuthUserContext from './context';
import { withFirebase } from '../Firebase';
import * as ROUTES from '../../constants/routes';

const withAuthorization = condition => Component => {
  class WithAuthorization extends React.Component {
    componentDidMount() {
      this.listener = firebase.auth.onAuthStateChanged(authUser => {
        if (!condition(authUser)) {
          this.props.history.push(ROUTES.SIGN_IN);
        }
      });
    }

    componentWillUnmount() {
      this.listener();
    }

    render() {
      return (
        <AuthUserContext.Consumer>
          {authUser =>
            condition(authUser) ? <Component {...this.props} /> : null
          }
        </AuthUserContext.Consumer>
      );
    }
  }

  return compose(
    withRouter,
    withFirebase,
  )(WithAuthorization);
};
```

```
export default withAuthorization;
```

The improvement in the render method was needed to avoid showing the protected page before the redirect happens. You want to show nothing if the authenticated user doesn't meet the condition's criteria. Then it's fine if the listener is too late to redirect the user, because the higher-order component didn't show the protected component.

Both routes are protected now, so we can render properties of the authenticated user in the AccountPage component without a null check for the authenticated user. You know the user should be there, otherwise the higher-order component would redirect to a public route.

src/components/Account/index.js

```
import React from 'react';

import { AuthUserContext, withAuthorization } from '../Session';
import { PasswordForgetForm } from '../PasswordForget';
import PasswordChangeForm from '../PasswordChange';

const AccountPage = () => (
  <AuthUserContext.Consumer>
    {authUser => (
      <div>
        <h1>Account: {authUser.email}</h1>
        <PasswordForgetForm />
        <PasswordChangeForm />
      </div>
    )}
  </AuthUserContext.Consumer>
);

const condition = authUser => !!authUser;

export default withAuthorization(condition)(AccountPage);
```

You can try it by signing out from your application and trying to access the */account* or */home* routes. Both should redirect you to the */signin* route. It should also redirect you automatically when you stay on one of the routes while you sign out.

You can imagine how this technique gives control over authorizations, not just by broader authorization rules, but more specific role-based and permission-based authorizations. For instance, an admin page available for users with the admin role could be protected as follows:

Code Playground

```
import React from 'react';

import * as ROLES from '../../constants/roles';

const AdminPage = () => (
  <div>
    <h1>Admin</h1>
    <p>
      Restricted area! Only users with the admin role are authorized.
    </p>
  </div>
);

const condition = authUser =>
  authUser && !!authUser.roles[ROLES.ADMIN];

export default withAuthorization(condition)(AdminPage);
```

Don't worry about this yet, because we'll implement a role-based authorization for this application later. For now, you have successfully implemented a full-fledged authentication mechanisms with Firebase in React, added neat features such as password reset and password change, and protected routes with dynamic authorization conditions.

Exercises:

- Research yourself how a role-based or permission-based authorization could be implemented.
- Confirm your source code for the last section[61]

---

[61]http://bit.ly/2Vop4SL

Firebase Realtime Database (1): Basic

So far, only Firebase knows about your users. There is no way to retrieve a single user or a list of users for your application from their authentication database. They are stored internally by Firebase to keep the authentication secure. That's good, because you are never involved in storing sensible data like passwords. However, you can introduce the Firebase realtime database to keep track of user entities yourself. It makes sense, because then you can associate other domain entities (e.g. a message, a book, an invoice) created by your users to your users. You should keep control over your users, even though Firebase takes care about all the sensible data. This section will explain how to store users in your realtime database in Firebase. First, initialize the realtime database API for your Firebase class as you did earlier for the authentication API:

src/components/Firebase/firebase.js

```
import app from 'firebase/app';
import 'firebase/auth';
import 'firebase/database';

const config = { ... };

class Firebase {
  constructor() {
    app.initializeApp(config);

    this.auth = app.auth();
    this.db = app.database();
  }

  // *** Auth API ***

  ...
}

export default Firebase;
```

Second, extend the interface for your Firebase class for the user entity. It defines two new functions: one to get a reference to a user by identifier (uid) and one to get a reference to all users:

src/components/Firebase/firebase.js

```
import app from 'firebase/app';
import 'firebase/auth';
import 'firebase/database';

const config = { ... };

class Firebase {
  constructor() {
    app.initializeApp(config);

    this.auth = app.auth();
    this.db = app.database();
  }

  // *** Auth API ***

  doCreateUserWithEmailAndPassword = (email, password) =>
    this.auth.createUserWithEmailAndPassword(email, password);

  doSignInWithEmailAndPassword = (email, password) =>
    this.auth.signInWithEmailAndPassword(email, password);

  doSignOut = () => this.auth.signOut();

  doPasswordReset = email => this.auth.sendPasswordResetEmail(email);

  doPasswordUpdate = password =>
    this.auth.currentUser.updatePassword(password);

  // *** User API ***

  user = uid => this.db.ref(`users/${uid}`);

  users = () => this.db.ref('users');
}

export default Firebase;
```

The paths in the `ref()` method match the location where your entities (users) will be stored in Firebase's realtime database API. If you delete a user at "users/5", the user with the identifier 5 will be removed from the database. If you create a new user at "users", Firebase creates the identifier for you and assigns all the information you pass for the user. The paths follow the REST philosophy[62] where every entity (e.g. user, message, book, author) is associated with a URI, and HTTP methods are used to create, update, delete and get entities. In Firebase, the RESTful URI becomes a simple path, and the HTTP methods become Firebase's API.

Exercises:

- Activate Firebase's Realtime Database[63] on your Firebase Dashboard
  - Set your Database Rules on your Firebase Project's Dashboard to { "rules": { ".read": true, ".write": true } } to give everyone read and write access for now.
- Read more about Firebase's realtime database setup for Web[64]
- Confirm your source code for the last section[65]

---

[62]https://en.wikipedia.org/wiki/Representational_state_transfer
[63]https://www.robinwieruch.de/firebase-tutorial/
[64]https://firebase.google.com/docs/database/web/start
[65]http://bit.ly/2VpDkdW

User Management with Firebase

Now, use these references in your React components to create and get users from Firebase's realtime database. The best place to add user creation is the SignUpForm component, as it is the most natural place to save users after signing up via the Firebase authentication API. Add another API request to create a user when the sign up is successful.

src/components/SignUp/index.js

```
...

class SignUpFormBase extends Component {
  constructor(props) {
    super(props);

    this.state = { ...INITIAL_STATE };
  }

  onSubmit = event => {
    const { username, email, passwordOne } = this.state;

    this.props.firebase
      .doCreateUserWithEmailAndPassword(email, passwordOne)
      .then(authUser => {
        // Create a user in your Firebase realtime database
        return this.props.firebase
          .user(authUser.user.uid)
          .set({
            username,
            email,
          });
      })
      .then(() => {
        this.setState({ ...INITIAL_STATE });
        this.props.history.push(ROUTES.HOME);
      })
      .catch(error => {
        this.setState({ error });
      });

    event.preventDefault();
  };
```

```
    . . .
}
```

```
. . .
```

There are two important things happening for a new sign up via the submit handler:

- (1) It creates a user in Firebase's internal authentication database that is only limited accessible.
- (2) If (1) was successful, it creates a user in Firebase's realtime database that is accessible.

To create a user in Firebase's realtime database, it uses the previously created reference from the Firebase class by providing the identifier (uid) of the user from Firebase's authentication database. Then the set() method can be used to provide data for this entity which is allocated for "users/uid". Finally, you can use the username as well to provide additional information about your user.

Note: It is fine to store user information in your own database. However, you should make sure not to store the password or any other sensible data of the user on your own. Firebase already deals with the authentication, so there is no need to store the password in your database. Many steps are necessary to secure sensible data (e.g. encryption), and it could be a security risk to perform it on your own.

After the second Firebase request that creates the user resolves successfully, the previous business logic takes place again: reset the local state and redirect to the home page. To verify the user creation is working, retrieve all the users from the realtime database in one of your other components. The admin page may be a good choice for it, because it can be used by admin users to manage the application-wide users later. First, make the admin page available via your Navigation component:

src/components/Navigation/index.js

```
. . .

const NavigationAuth = () => (
  <ul>
    <li>
      <Link to={ROUTES.LANDING}>Landing</Link>
    </li>
    <li>
      <Link to={ROUTES.HOME}>Home</Link>
    </li>
    <li>
      <Link to={ROUTES.ACCOUNT}>Account</Link>
    </li>
    <li>
      <Link to={ROUTES.ADMIN}>Admin</Link>
```

```
      </li>
      <li>
        <SignOutButton />
      </li>
    </ul>
  );
```

. . .

Next, the AdminPage component's `componentDidMount()` lifecycle method in *src/components/Admin/index.js* is the perfect place to fetch users from your Firebase realtime database API:

src/components/Admin/index.js

```
import React, { Component } from 'react';

import { withFirebase } from '../Firebase';

class AdminPage extends Component {
  constructor(props) {
    super(props);

    this.state = {
      loading: false,
      users: {},
    };
  }

  componentDidMount() {
    this.setState({ loading: true });

    this.props.firebase.users().on('value', snapshot => {
      this.setState({
        users: snapshot.val(),
        loading: false,
      });
    });
  }

  render() {
    return (
      <div>
        <h1>Admin</h1>
      </div>
```

```
    );
  }
}


export default withFirebase(AdminPage);
```

We are using the users reference from our Firebase class to attach a listener. The listener is called on( ), which receives a type and a callback function. The on( ) method registers a continuous listener that triggers every time something has changed, the once( ) method registers a listener that would be called only once. In this scenario, we are interested to keep the latest list of users though.

Since the users are objects rather than lists when they are retrieved from the Firebase database, you have to restructure them as lists (arrays), which makes it easier to display them later:

src/components/Admin/index.js

```
...

class AdminPage extends Component {
  constructor(props) {
    super(props);

    this.state = {
      loading: false,
      users: [],
    };
  }

  componentDidMount() {
    this.setState({ loading: true });

    this.props.firebase.users().on('value', snapshot => {
      const usersObject = snapshot.val();

      const usersList = Object.keys(usersObject).map(key => ({
        ...usersObject[key],
        uid: key,
      }));

      this.setState({
        users: usersList,
        loading: false,
      });
    });
```

```
  }


    ...
}
```

```
export default withFirebase(AdminPage);
```

Remember to remove the listener to avoid memory leaks from using the same reference with the off() method:

src/components/Admin/index.js

```
...

class AdminPage extends Component {
  ...

  componentWillUnmount() {
    this.props.firebase.users().off();
  }


    ...
}
```

```
export default withFirebase(AdminPage);
```

Render your list of users in the AdminPage component or in a child component. In this case, we are using a child component:

src/components/Admin/index.js

```
...

class AdminPage extends Component {
  ...

  render() {
    const { users, loading } = this.state;

    return (
      <div>
        <h1>Admin</h1>

        {loading && <div>Loading ...</div>}
```

```
        <UserList users={users} />
      </div>
    );
  }
}

const UserList = ({ users }) => (
  <ul>
    {users.map(user => (
      <li key={user.uid}>
        <span>
          <strong>ID:</strong> {user.uid}
        </span>
        <span>
          <strong>E-Mail:</strong> {user.email}
        </span>
        <span>
          <strong>Username:</strong> {user.username}
        </span>
      </li>
    ))}
  </ul>
);
```

```
export default withFirebase(AdminPage);
```

You have gained full control of your users now. It is possible to create and retrieve users from your realtime database. You can decide whether this is a one-time call to the Firebase realtime database, or if you want to continuously listen for updates as well.

Exercises:

- Read more about how to read and write data to Firebase's realtime database[66]
- Confirm your source code for the last section[67]

---

[66]https://firebase.google.com/docs/database/web/read-and-write
[67]http://bit.ly/2VmRegY

Authorization (2): Roles and Permissions

So far, you've used broad authorization rules that check user authentication, where the dedicated authorization higher-order component redirects them to the login page if the user is not authenticated. In this section, you will apply a more specific authorization mechanism. It works with roles (e.g. Admin, Author) assigned to a user, but also with permissions (e.g. user is allowed to write an article). Again, if the user doesn't fit a role for the authorization condition in your authorization higher-order component, the user will be redirected. Let's revisit the *src/components/Session/withAuthorization.js* higher-order component we have implemented thus far:

src/components/Session/withAuthorization.js

```
import React from 'react';
import { withRouter } from 'react-router-dom';
import { compose } from 'recompose';

import AuthUserContext from './context';
import { withFirebase } from '../Firebase';
import * as ROUTES from '../../constants/routes';

const withAuthorization = condition => Component => {
  class WithAuthorization extends React.Component {
    componentDidMount() {
      this.listener = this.props.firebase.auth.onAuthStateChanged(
        authUser => {
          if (!condition(authUser)) {
            this.props.history.push(ROUTES.SIGN_IN);
          }
        },
      );
    }

    componentWillUnmount() {
      this.listener();
    }

    render() {
      return (
```

```
      <AuthUserContext.Consumer>
        {authUser =>
          condition(authUser) ? <Component {...this.props} /> : null
        }
      </AuthUserContext.Consumer>
    );
  }
}

return compose(
  withRouter,
  withFirebase,
)(WithAuthorization);
};

export default withAuthorization;
```

The Firebase listener always gives us the recent authenticated user. We don't know if the user is null though, so we deployed broader authorization rules for a few routes (e.g. */home*) of the application. If a user is not authenticated, we redirect the user to the login page.

Code Playground

```
const condition = authUser => !!authUser;
```

Now we can go a step further and check for a user's role or permission:

Code Playground

```
const condition = authUser =>
  authUser && !!authUser.roles[ROLES.ADMIN];
```

Assigning properties like an object of roles to authenticated users is a straightforward task. However, as we learned in previous sections, authenticated users are managed internally by Firebase. We are not able to alter user properties, so we manage them in Firebase's realtime database. If you go to your Firebase project's dashboard, you can see that users are managed in the Authentication and Database tabs. We introduced the latter to keep track of the users and assign them additional properties ourselves.

This section is split up into three parts:

- Assign a user on sign up a roles (e.g. admin role) property.
- Merge the authenticated user and database user so they can be authorized with their roles in the authorization higher-order component.

- Showcase a role authorization for one of our routes (e.g. only allowed for admin users).

Firebase has an official way to introduce roles to your authenticated user. I am not very comfortable with it, though, because it uses lots of Firebase internals and increases the effect of vendor lock-ins. Instead, I prefer storing roles directly into the user entities in the Firebase database. This way, you'll have an easier time migrating away from Firebase if you decide to roll out a backend application with a database.

Database Users with Roles

We'll use multiple roles because users may have more than one role in the application or system. For instance, a user could be an admin, but also an author with access to admin and author areas. Let's assign a `roles` property to our users when they are created in the realtime database on sign-up. First, we'll track a checkbox state for this type of role in our component:

src/components/SignUp/index.js

```
const INITIAL_STATE = {
  username: '',
  email: '',
  passwordOne: '',
  passwordTwo: '',
  isAdmin: false,
  error: null,
};
```

Next, add a checkbox to toggle the user role in the UI:

src/components/SignUp/index.js

```
class SignUpFormBase extends Component {

  ...

  onChangeCheckbox = event => {
    this.setState({ [event.target.name]: event.target.checked });
  };

  render() {
    const {
      username,
      email,
      passwordOne,
      passwordTwo,
      isAdmin,
      error,
    } = this.state;

    ...

    return (
      <form onSubmit={this.onSubmit}>
```

```
  . . .
    <label>
      Admin:
      <input
        name="isAdmin"
        type="checkbox"
        checked={isAdmin}
        onChange={this.onChangeCheckbox}
      />
    </label>
    <button disabled={isInvalid} type="submit">
      Sign Up
    </button>

    {error && <p>{error.message}</p>}
    </form>
  );
}
}
```

. . .

We don't want to grant any user the power to sign up as admin, but we'll keep it simple for now, and you can decide which circumstances prompt you to assign roles to users later. Next, add the roles property to your user when they are created in the database. Since we need an object of roles, we'll initialize it as an empty object and add conditional roles to it:

src/components/SignUp/index.js

```
import React, { Component } from 'react';
import { Link, withRouter } from 'react-router-dom';
import { compose } from 'recompose';

import { withFirebase } from '../Firebase';
import * as ROUTES from '../../constants/routes';
import * as ROLES from '../../constants/roles';

. . .

class SignUpFormBase extends Component {
  . . .

  onSubmit = event => {
    const { username, email, passwordOne, isAdmin } = this.state;
```

```
  const roles = {};

  if (isAdmin) {
    roles[ROLES.ADMIN] = ROLES.ADMIN;
  }

  this.props.firebase
    .doCreateUserWithEmailAndPassword(email, passwordOne)
    .then(authUser => {
      // Create a user in your Firebase realtime database
      return this.props.firebase
        .user(authUser.user.uid)
        .set({
          username,
          email,
          roles,
        })
    })
    .then(() => {
      this.setState({ ...INITIAL_STATE });
      this.props.history.push(ROUTES.HOME);
    })
    .catch(error => {
      this.setState({ error });
    });

  event.preventDefault();
};


  ...
}


...
```

Next, collect all your roles in the *src/constants/roles.js* file we just imported in the previous step. It can be used to assign roles as you did before, but also to protect routes later on.

src/constants/roles.js

```
export const ADMIN = 'ADMIN';
```

You should be able to create users with admin privileges now. Next we'll cover how to merge this user from our database with the authenticated user from the Firebase authentication.

How to merge authenticated user with database user?

Since we need to check the roles only in the authorization higher-order component, it's best to merge the authentication user and database user in this component before checking for its privileges (roles, permissions).

src/components/Session/withAuthorization.js

```
...

const withAuthorization = condition => Component => {
  class WithAuthorization extends React.Component {
    componentDidMount() {
      this.listener = this.props.firebase.auth.onAuthStateChanged(
        authUser => {
          if (authUser) {
            this.props.firebase
              .user(authUser.uid)
              .once('value')
              .then(snapshot => {
                const dbUser = snapshot.val();

                // default empty roles
                if (!dbUser.roles) {
                  dbUser.roles = {};
                }

                // merge auth and db user
                authUser = {
                  uid: authUser.uid,
                  email: authUser.email,
                  ...dbUser,
                };

                if (!condition(authUser)) {
                  this.props.history.push(ROUTES.SIGN_IN);
                }
              });
          } else {
            this.props.history.push(ROUTES.SIGN_IN);
          }
        },
      );
```

```
    }

      . . .

  }

  . . .

};
```

. . .

When the authenticated user changes, the function within the listener is called. If the user is null, it redirects. If the user is not null, we will get the database user with the help of the authenticated user's unique identifier, and then we merge everything from the database user with the unique identifier and email from the authenticated user. You may need more properties from the authenticated user later, but at this point the unique identifier and the email are sufficient. As we did before, we are running our conditional check to see if the user is authorized or not. However, now we have all the properties from the database user (e.g. roles) at our disposal. If the conditions are not met, we redirect the user. If the conditions are met, the user stays on the page component enhanced by the authorization higher-order component.

We've covered merging the user in the authorization higher-order component. Next, we'll consider the authentication higher-order component that provides authentication for all our components. Maybe we want to show something to the user based on their level of authentication like a link to admin page in the navigation. Let's implement the merging in this higher-order component, too:

src/components/Session/withAuthentication.js

. . .

```
const withAuthentication = Component => {
  class WithAuthentication extends React.Component {
    componentDidMount() {
      this.listener = this.props.firebase.auth.onAuthStateChanged(
        authUser => {
          if (authUser) {
            this.props.firebase
              .user(authUser.uid)
              .once('value')
              .then(snapshot => {
                const dbUser = snapshot.val();

                // default empty roles
                if (!dbUser.roles) {
                  dbUser.roles = {};
```

```
        }

        // merge auth and db user
        authUser = {
          uid: authUser.uid,
          email: authUser.email,
          ...dbUser,
        };

        this.setState({ authUser });
      });
    } else {
      this.setState({ authUser: null });
    }
  },
  );
}

...

}


...

};


...
```

Now the authenticated user is provided via React's Context API extended with the database user to all our components. As you may have noticed, the implementation was quite repetitive to the authorization higher-order component. The only thing we changed was the local state usage instead of the redirects. Let's see how we can extract the common implementation to our Firebase class without touching the implementation details with the local state (authentication higher-order component) and the redirection (authorization higher-order component).

src/components/Firebase/firebase.js

```
...


class Firebase {
  ...


  // *** Auth API ***


  ...
```

```
// *** Merge Auth and DB User API *** //

onAuthUserListener = (next, fallback) =>
  this.auth.onAuthStateChanged(authUser => {
    if (authUser) {
      this.user(authUser.uid)
        .once('value')
        .then(snapshot => {
          const dbUser = snapshot.val();

          // default empty roles
          if (!dbUser.roles) {
            dbUser.roles = {};
          }

          // merge auth and db user
          authUser = {
            uid: authUser.uid,
            email: authUser.email,
            ...dbUser,
          };

          next(authUser);
        });
    } else {
      fallback();
    }
  });

// *** User API ***

...
}


export default Firebase;
```

Observe which common implementation details were taken from the two higher-order components. The only thing changed in this extracted function are the next() and fallback() callback functions. This is where we can implement the specific implementation details of every higher-order component (local state for authentication, redirect for authorization) that uses this new method. Let's use this function first in the authentication higher-order component and provide both callback functions as "next" and "fallback":

src/components/Session/withAuthentication.js

```
...

const withAuthentication = Component => {
  class WithAuthentication extends React.Component {
    ...

    componentDidMount() {
      this.listener = this.props.firebase.onAuthUserListener(
        authUser => {
          this.setState({ authUser });
        },
        () => {
          this.setState({ authUser: null });
        },
      );
    }

    ...

  }

  ...

};

...
```

The higher-order component uses this new method from the Firebase instance, providing only two callback functions as parameters. The first callback function is used for the merged user; the second is used when the authenticated user is null. Let's use the new method in the authorization higher-order component as well:

src/components/Session/withAuthorization.js

```
...

const withAuthorization = condition => Component => {
  class WithAuthorization extends React.Component {
    ...

    componentDidMount() {
      this.listener = this.props.firebase.onAuthUserListener(
        authUser => {
          if (!condition(authUser)) {
```

```
            this.props.history.push(ROUTES.SIGN_IN);
          }
        },
        () => this.props.history.push(ROUTES.SIGN_IN),
      );
    }


    . . .

  }


  . . .

};


. . .
```

We extracted the business logic that merges authentication user and database user to the Firebase class, made it available as method on the class instance, and used it in both higher-order components. Since we can provide two callback functions to this new method, which are executed based on whether the user is authenticated or not, each higher-order component gains control over what happens afterward. The authorization higher-order component cares about redirects, while the authentication higher-order component cares about storing the merged user in the local state and distributing it to other components via React's Context Provider component.

Authorize a Firebase User based on a Role

Now we need to check whether our role-based authorization is working after all. The admin page is the best place to deploy a role-based authorization, because so far it is open for everyone and not secured.

src/components/Admin/index.js

```
import React, { Component } from 'react';
import { compose } from 'recompose';

import { withFirebase } from '../Firebase';
import { withAuthorization } from '../Session';
import * as ROLES from '../../constants/roles';

class AdminPage extends Component {
  ...

  render() {
    const { users, loading } = this.state;

    return (
      <div>
        <h1>Admin</h1>
        <p>
          The Admin Page is accessible by every signed in admin user.
        </p>

        {loading && <div>Loading ...</div>}

        <UserList users={users} />
      </div>
    );
  }
}

...

const condition = authUser =>
  authUser && !!authUser.roles[ROLES.ADMIN];

export default compose(
  withAuthorization(condition),
```

```
  withFirebase,
)(AdminPage);
```

If you try to access the admin page as non-authenticated user or as non-admin user without the necessary role, it redirects you to the login page. If you access it as user with admin privileges, you should be able to see the desired content. The authorization higher-order component made this possible.

Next, we'll secure the route to the admin page in the Navigation component. That's where the (merged) authenticated user from the authentication higher-order component comes in. Using React's Context in this higher-order component, you can access the extended authenticated user:

src/components/Navigation/index.js

```
...

import { AuthUserContext } from '../Session';
import SignOutButton from '../SignOut';
import * as ROUTES from '../../constants/routes';
import * as ROLES from '../../constants/roles';

const Navigation = () => (
  <AuthUserContext.Consumer>
    {authUser =>
      authUser ? (
        <NavigationAuth authUser={authUser} />
      ) : (
        <NavigationNonAuth />
      )
    }
  </AuthUserContext.Consumer>
);

const NavigationAuth = ({ authUser }) => (
  <ul>
    <li>
      <Link to={ROUTES.LANDING}>Landing</Link>
    </li>
    <li>
      <Link to={ROUTES.HOME}>Home</Link>
    </li>
    <li>
      <Link to={ROUTES.ACCOUNT}>Account</Link>
    </li>
```

```
    {!!authUser.roles[ROLES.ADMIN] && (
      <li>
        <Link to={ROUTES.ADMIN}>Admin</Link>
      </li>
    )}
    <li>
      <SignOutButton />
    </li>
  </ul>
);

const NavigationNonAuth = () => (
  <ul>
    <li>
      <Link to={ROUTES.LANDING}>Landing</Link>
    </li>
    <li>
      <Link to={ROUTES.SIGN_IN}>Sign In</Link>
    </li>
  </ul>
);

export default Navigation;
```

You have successfully assigned roles to your users, merged authentication user with the database user in your higher-order components, and applied authorization rules with redirects and conditional rendering in your application. Everything that is added to the database user will be available when you launch your application, and you've set properties for the Firebase user.

Exercises:

- Walk through a scenario where the role-based authorization could be replaced with a permission-based authorization (e.g. `authUser.permissions.canEditUser`).
- Confirm your source code for the last section[68]

---

[68]http://bit.ly/2VneMT2

Session Persistence

Previously, we implemented authentication for this Firebase in React application. Along the way, we added authorization with roles. You may have experienced a flicker every time you reload/refresh your browser, because the application doesn't know from the start if a user is authenticated or not since the authenticated user is null. It will happen until Firebase figures out there is an authenticated user and calls the function in the listener of the authentication higher-order component:

src/components/Session/withAuthentication.js

```
import React from 'react';

import AuthUserContext from './context';
import { withFirebase } from '../Firebase';

const withAuthentication = Component => {
  class WithAuthentication extends React.Component {
    constructor(props) {
      super(props);

      this.state = {
        authUser: null,
      };
    }

    componentDidMount() {
      this.listener = this.props.firebase.onAuthUserListener(
        authUser => {
          this.setState({ authUser });
        },
        () => {
          this.setState({ authUser: null });
        },
      );
    }

    componentWillUnmount() {
      this.listener();
    }
```

```
  render() {
    return (
      <AuthUserContext.Provider value={this.state.authUser}>
        <Component {...this.props} />
      </AuthUserContext.Provider>
    );
  }
}

  return withFirebase(WithAuthentication);
};


export default withAuthentication;
```

After the Firebase authentication listener is invoked for the first time, the authenticated user may be there, because Firebase has its internal state for auth persistence. Also, the routes are made visible in the Navigation component due to the authenticated user being there now. While it's good that Firebase keeps the state of the authenticated user, the UI glitch in the beginning hurts the user experience. Let's avoid this using the browser's local storage[69] for the authenticated user:

src/components/Session/withAuthentication.js

```
...

const withAuthentication = Component => {
  class WithAuthentication extends React.Component {
    constructor(props) {
      super(props);

      this.state = {
        authUser: null,
      };
    }

    componentDidMount() {
      this.listener = this.props.firebase.onAuthUserListener(
        authUser => {
          localStorage.setItem('authUser', JSON.stringify(authUser));
          this.setState({ authUser });
        },
        () => {
          localStorage.removeItem('authUser');
```

---

[69]https://www.robinwieruch.de/local-storage-react/

```
            this.setState({ authUser: null });
        },
      );
    }


    ...

  }


  ...

};


...
```

Every time Firebase's listener is invoked, the authenticated user is not only stored in the local state, ready to be passed to React's Context API, but it's also stored in the browser's local storage. You can use the local storage's API with setItem and removeItem to store and delete something identified by a key. You also need to format the authenticated user to JSON before you can put it into the local storage of the browser.

The flicker is still there, because we're not really taking advantage of having the authenticated user earlier at our disposal. Let's change this by retrieving it from the local storage in the higher-order component's constructor earlier:

src/components/Session/withAuthentication.js

```
...

const withAuthentication = Component => {
  class WithAuthentication extends React.Component {
    constructor(props) {
      super(props);

      this.state = {
        authUser: JSON.parse(localStorage.getItem('authUser')),
      };
    }


    ...

  }


  ...

};


...
```

If there is no auth user in the local storage, the local state will stay null and everything will remain as before. However, if the authenticated user is in the local storage because it was stored via our Firebase listener's function, we can use it in the component's constructor. Since the format of the authenticated user in the local storage is JSON, we need to transform it into a JavaScript object again. Ultimately, someone using our application can refresh the browser, but also close the browser/tab and open it after a while, and it will still see them as an authenticated user.

Try the application again and verify that the flicker is gone. Also all the conditional routes and pages that are protected with a conditional rendering (e.g. Navigation component) or authorization (e.g. HomePage component) should be there immediately. The authentication higher-order component can pass the authenticated user with its first render via React's Context API to all other components.

Exercises:

- Read more about Auth Persistence in Firebase[70]
- Explore using the Browser's Session Storage instead of the Local Storage to give the authenticated user an expiration date.
- Confirm your source code for the last section[71]

---

[70]https://firebase.google.com/docs/auth/web/auth-state-persistence
[71]http://bit.ly/2VoNhZj

Social Logins

So far, you have used a email/password combination to authenticated with the application. Firebase offers more than this sign in method. If you take a closer look at their documentation, you can find social sign in methods for Google, Facebook, Twitter and others. In this section, I want to show you how to use these social logins to give users access to your application. It removes lots of friction to use your application, because not everyone wants to create a new account from scratch. Rather people tend more and more to use social logins for services and products.

Note: The following sections show API keys, secrets, URIs and other sensible data that you shouldn't share with other people. They should be kept secret. That's why all the sensible data shown in the following sections is fake.

Firebase has the restriction to allow only one E-Mail address per user. If you try to use another sign in method next to the default email/password sign in method, you may see the following error: *"An account already exists with the same email address but different sign in credentials. Sign in using a provider associated with this email address."* It's because your E-Mail address from your Google account may be the same as for Facebook account or your default email/password combination. In order to overcome this behavior, only for this section though, you can deactivate it in your Firebase dashboard on the Authentication tab. There you can allow more than one account for the same E-Mail address:

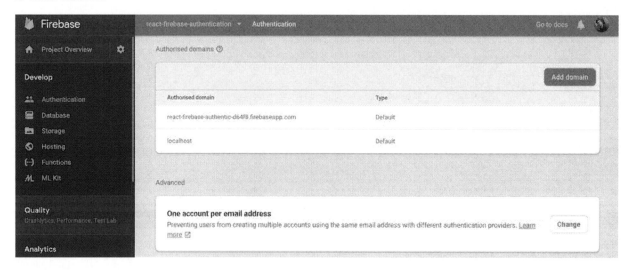

Keep in mind that we will revert this configuration later though, because you don't want to create a dedicated user account for each social login in the end. It would mean that someone creating content with their Facebook social login wouldn't own the content with their Google social login anymore, because it's a different account. However, let's create the social logins this way first and see how we can merge them into one account later.

Troubleshoot

There are a few errors that could show up for while setting up Google, Facebook or Twitter social logins for your application. First, understand the error message yourself and try to figure out the fix for it. However, I want to document a few things I have noticed myself and how I fixed them. If you encounter any of these issues, check again this troubleshooting area. Let's see what kind of errors we have and how to fix them:

Info: *The current domain is not authorized for OAuth operations. This will prevent signInWith-Popup, signInWithRedirect, linkWithPopup and linkWithRedirect from working. Add your domain (localhost) to the OAuth redirect domains list in the Firebase console -> Auth section -> Sign in methodÂ tab.*

On your Firebase dashboard, you will find an Authentication tab to get a list of all your authenticated users, sign up methods and other configuration. Click the Authentication tab and scroll down to "Authorised domains" and add "localhost" there. Then your development domain should be authorized to perform the Auth operations with third-parties.

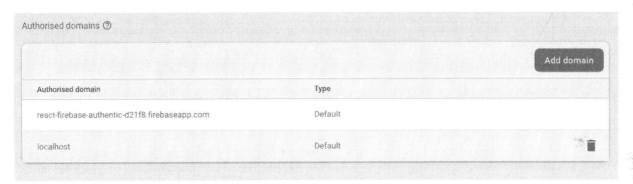

It's a mandatory configuration for most of Firebase's sign in methods. However, it can be that this alone doesn't help and you need to perform further configuration. Therefore, visit Google's Developer Console[72] and select your Firebase project in the top-level navigation and navigate to "Credentials" afterward.

There you will see configuration for "API keys" and "OAuth 2.0 client IDs". In "API keys", edit "Browser key (auto created by Google Service)" and add localhost and the authDomain from your project's configuration in "Accept requests from these HTTP referrers (websites)".

---

[72]https://console.developers.google.com/apis/credentials

Application restrictions   API restrictions

Application restrictions specify which web sites, IP addresses or apps can use this key. You can set one restriction type per key.

Application restrictions

○ None

◉ HTTP referrers (websites)

○ IP addresses (web servers, cron jobs, etc.)

○ Android apps

○ iOS apps

Accept requests from these HTTP referrers (websites) (Optional)
Use asterisks for wildcards. If you leave this blank, requests will be accepted from any referrer. Be sure to add referrers before using this key in production.

| localhost | × |

| react-firebase-authentic-d21f8.firebaseapp.com | × |

| https://*.example.com/* | |

Note: It may take up to 5 minutes for settings to take effect.

Next, in "OAuth 2.0 client IDs", edit "Web client (auto created by Google Service)" and add localhost and the authDomain from your project's configuration in "Authorised JavaScript origins".

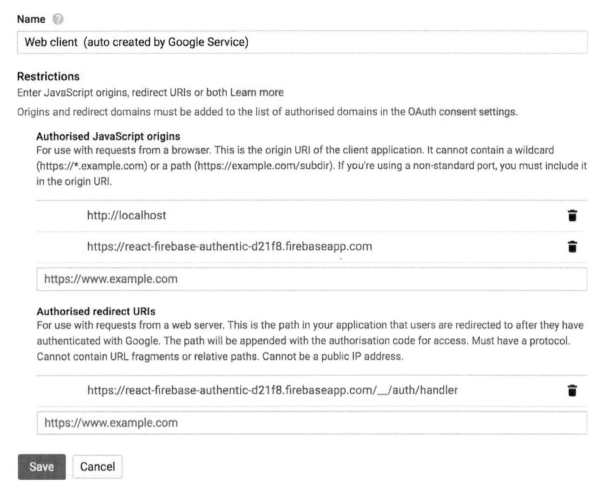

It can take some time until the changes are propagated through Google's services (e.g. Firebase). But then all third-parties should be authorised to access your Firebase project.

Google Social Login

Before we can start to code the social login for Google with Firebase in React, we need to enable it as sign in method on our Firebase project's dashboard. You can find all your sign in methods under the "Authentication" tab.

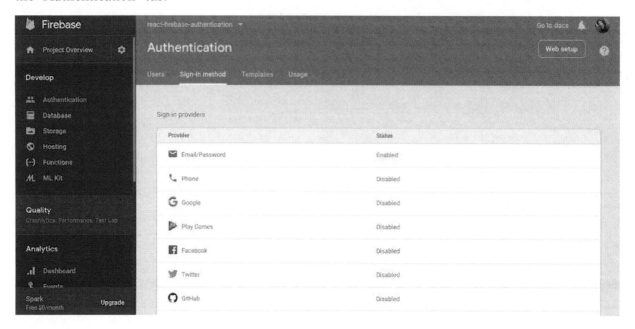

Afterward, we are able to implement the social login in our code. In the Firebase class that's our interface between our React application and the Firebase API, add the Google Authentication Provider and the class method to sign in with Google by using the provider:

src/components/Firebase/firebase.js

```
...

class Firebase {
  constructor() {
    app.initializeApp(config);

    this.auth = app.auth();
    this.db = app.database();

    this.googleProvider = new app.auth.GoogleAuthProvider();
  }

  // *** Auth API ***

  doCreateUserWithEmailAndPassword = (email, password) =>
```

```
      this.auth.createUserWithEmailAndPassword(email, password);

  doSignInWithEmailAndPassword = (email, password) =>
    this.auth.signInWithEmailAndPassword(email, password);

  doSignInWithGoogle = () =>
    this.auth.signInWithPopup(this.googleProvider);

  doSignOut = () => this.auth.signOut();


  ...
}

export default Firebase;
```

On your sign in page, add a new component for a sign in with Google next to your email/password sign in:

src/components/SignIn/index.js

```
...

const SignInPage = () => (
  <div>
    <h1>SignIn</h1>
    <SignInForm />
    <SignInGoogle />
    <PasswordForgetLink />
    <SignUpLink />
  </div>
);

...
```

Now implement the complete new form component in this same file for the Google sign in:

src/components/SignIn/index.js

```
...

class SignInGoogleBase extends Component {
  constructor(props) {
    super(props);

    this.state = { error: null };
  }

  onSubmit = event => {
    this.props.firebase
      .doSignInWithGoogle()
      .then(socialAuthUser => {
        this.setState({ error: null });
        this.props.history.push(ROUTES.HOME);
      })
      .catch(error => {
        this.setState({ error });
      });

    event.preventDefault();
  };

  render() {
    const { error } = this.state;

    return (
      <form onSubmit={this.onSubmit}>
        <button type="submit">Sign In with Google</button>

        {error && <p>{error.message}</p>}
      </form>
    );
  }
}

...
```

On submit the form component uses the new Google sign in method given by our Firebase's class instance. In order to pass Firebase and all other required configuration (e.g. history for a redirect after login) to this component, enhance it with all the needed higher-order components:

src/components/SignIn/index.js

```
...

const SignInForm = compose(
  withRouter,
  withFirebase,
)(SignInFormBase);

const SignInGoogle = compose(
  withRouter,
  withFirebase,
)(SignInGoogleBase);

export default SignInPage;

export { SignInForm, SignInGoogle };
```

So far, that should do the trick for the sign in with Google sign in method. You will have an authenticated user afterward, but what's missing is the database user that you have to create yourself. It's similar to the sign up (registration) in the SignUpForm component:

src/components/SignIn/index.js

```
...

class SignInGoogleBase extends Component {
  ...

  onSubmit = event => {
    this.props.firebase
      .doSignInWithGoogle()
      .then(socialAuthUser => {
        // Create a user in your Firebase Realtime Database too
        return this.props.firebase
          .user(socialAuthUser.user.uid)
          .set({
            username: socialAuthUser.user.displayName,
            email: socialAuthUser.user.email,
            roles: {},
          });
      })
      .then(() => {
        this.setState({ error: null });
```

```
        this.props.history.push(ROUTES.HOME);
      })
      .catch(error => {
        this.setState({ error });
      });

    event.preventDefault();
  };

  ...
}


...
```

In this scenario, every time a user signs in with Google, a new user with this stable id coming from the social login is created in your database. Basically if a user signs in twice with the same social login, the old user gets overridden. This can be a desired behavior, because maybe a user has changed their username on Google and want to see it reflected in your applications's database too. If you don't want to have this behavior and only create the user once with a social login, make use of the `socialuser.additionalUserInfo.isNewUser` property to only create a new user when signing in with Google for the first time.

Exercises:

- Read more about the Google Social Login[73]
- Check your Firebase's Dashboard Authentication/Database tabs to manage your users (e.g. manually remove users).
- Confirm your source code for the last section[74]

---

[73]https://firebase.google.com/docs/auth/web/google-signin
[74]http://bit.ly/2VuH8eh

Facebook Social Login

Identical to the previous social login, enable the sign in method on your Firebase dashboard for Facebook. The Facebook social login expects an App ID and and App Secret. You can get these by creating a new Facebook App with your Facebook Account for this Firebase in React application[75]. Afterward, you can find the App ID and App Secret for your new Facebook App.

Afterward, we are able to implement the social login in our code. In the Firebase class, add the Facebook Authentication Provider and the class method to sign in with Facebook by using the provider:

src/components/Firebase/firebase.js

```
...

class Firebase {
  constructor() {
    app.initializeApp(config);

    this.auth = app.auth();
    this.db = app.database();

    this.googleProvider = new app.auth.GoogleAuthProvider();
    this.facebookProvider = new app.auth.FacebookAuthProvider();
  }

  // *** Auth API ***

  doCreateUserWithEmailAndPassword = (email, password) =>
    this.auth.createUserWithEmailAndPassword(email, password);

  doSignInWithEmailAndPassword = (email, password) =>
    this.auth.signInWithEmailAndPassword(email, password);

  doSignInWithGoogle = () =>
    this.auth.signInWithPopup(this.googleProvider);

  doSignInWithFacebook = () =>
    this.auth.signInWithPopup(this.facebookProvider);

  doSignOut = () => this.auth.signOut();

  ...
```

---

[75]https://www.robinwieruch.de/firebase-facebook-login

```
}

export default Firebase;
```

On your sign in page, add a new component for a sign in with Facebook next to your email/password and Google sign ins:

src/components/SignIn/index.js

```
...

const SignInPage = () => (
  <div>
    <h1>SignIn</h1>
    <SignInForm />
    <SignInGoogle />
    <SignInFacebook />
    <PasswordForgetLink />
    <SignUpLink />
  </div>
);

...
```

Now implement the complete new form component in this same file for the Facebook sign in:

src/components/SignIn/index.js

```
...

class SignInFacebookBase extends Component {
  constructor(props) {
    super(props);

    this.state = { error: null };
  }

  onSubmit = event => {
    this.props.firebase
      .doSignInWithFacebook()
      .then(socialAuthUser => {
        this.setState({ error: null });
        this.props.history.push(ROUTES.HOME);
      })
```

```
      .catch(error => {
        this.setState({ error });
      });

    event.preventDefault();
  };

  render() {
    const { error } = this.state;

    return (
      <form onSubmit={this.onSubmit}>
        <button type="submit">Sign In with Facebook</button>

        {error && <p>{error.message}</p>}
      </form>
    );
  }
}
```

`...`

On submit the form component uses the new Facebook sign in method given by our Firebase's class instance. In order to pass Firebase and all other required configuration to this component, enhance it with all the needed higher-order components:

src/components/SignIn/index.js

`...`

```
const SignInGoogle = compose(
  withRouter,
  withFirebase,
)(SignInGoogleBase);

const SignInFacebook = compose(
  withRouter,
  withFirebase,
)(SignInFacebookBase);

export default SignInPage;

export { SignInForm, SignInGoogle, SignInFacebook };
```

You will have an authenticated user afterward, but what's missing again is the database user that
you have to create yourself:

src/components/SignIn/index.js

```
...

class SignInFacebookBase extends Component {
  ...

  onSubmit = event => {
    this.props.firebase
      .doSignInWithFacebook()
      .then(socialAuthUser => {
        // Create a user in your Firebase Realtime Database too
        return this.props.firebase
          .user(socialAuthUser.user.uid)
          .set({
            username: socialAuthUser.additionalUserInfo.profile.name,
            email: socialAuthUser.additionalUserInfo.profile.email,
            roles: {},
          });
      })
      .then(() => {
        this.setState({ error: null });
        this.props.history.push(ROUTES.HOME);
      })
      .catch(error => {
        this.setState({ error });
      });

    event.preventDefault();
  };

  ...
}

...
```

Again, every time a user signs in with Facebook, a new user with this stable id coming from the social
login is created in your database. Basically if a user signs in twice with the same social login, the old
user gets overridden. You can optionally make use of the `socialuser.additionalUserInfo.isNewUser`
property to only create a new user when signing in with Facebook for the first time.

Exercises:

- Read more about the Facebook Social Login[76]
- Figure out whether there is a way to interact with Facebook's API afterward, because the `socialUser` has an `accessToken` in its `credentials` object.
- Like my Facebook[77] page to receive latest tutorials for web developers.
- Confirm your source code for the last section[78]

---

[76]https://firebase.google.com/docs/auth/web/facebook-login
[77]https://www.facebook.com/rwieruch/
[78]http://bit.ly/2VuH8eh

Twitter Social Login

Identical to the previous social logins, enable the sign in method on your Firebase dashboard for Twitter. The Twitter social login expects an API key and API secret. You can get these by creating a new Twitter App with your Twitter Account for this Firebase in React application[79]. Afterward, you can find the API key and API secret for your new Twitter App.

Now, we are able to implement the social login in our code. In the Firebase class, add the Twitter Authentication Provider and the class method to sign in with Twitter by using the provider:

src/components/Firebase/firebase.js

```
...

class Firebase {
  constructor() {
    app.initializeApp(config);

    this.auth = app.auth();
    this.db = app.database();

    this.googleProvider = new app.auth.GoogleAuthProvider();
    this.facebookProvider = new app.auth.FacebookAuthProvider();
    this.twitterProvider = new app.auth.TwitterAuthProvider();
  }

  // *** Auth API ***

  ...

  doSignInWithGoogle = () =>
    this.auth.signInWithPopup(this.googleProvider);

  doSignInWithFacebook = () =>
    this.auth.signInWithPopup(this.facebookProvider);

  doSignInWithTwitter = () =>
    this.auth.signInWithPopup(this.twitterProvider);

  doSignOut = () => this.auth.signOut();

  ...
}
```

[79]https://www.robinwieruch.de/firebase-twitter-login

```
export default Firebase;
```

On your sign in page, add a new component for a sign in with Twitter next to your email/password, Google and Facebook sign ins:

src/components/SignIn/index.js

```
...

const SignInPage = () => (
  <div>
    <h1>SignIn</h1>
    <SignInForm />
    <SignInGoogle />
    <SignInFacebook />
    <SignInTwitter />
    <PasswordForgetLink />
    <SignUpLink />
  </div>
);

...
```

Now implement the complete new form component in this same file for the Twitter sign in:

src/components/SignIn/index.js

```
...

class SignInTwitterBase extends Component {
  constructor(props) {
    super(props);

    this.state = { error: null };
  }

  onSubmit = event => {
    this.props.firebase
      .doSignInWithTwitter()
      .then(socialAuthUser => {
        this.setState({ error: null });
        this.props.history.push(ROUTES.HOME);
      })
```

```
      .catch(error => {
        this.setState({ error });
      });

    event.preventDefault();
  };

  render() {
    const { error } = this.state;

    return (
      <form onSubmit={this.onSubmit}>
        <button type="submit">Sign In with Twitter</button>

        {error && <p>{error.message}</p>}
      </form>
    );
  }
}
```

```
...
```

On submit the form component uses the new Twitter sign in method given by our Firebase's class instance. In order to pass Firebase and all other required configuration to this component, enhance it with all the needed higher-order components:

src/components/SignIn/index.js

```
...

const SignInFacebook = compose(
  withRouter,
  withFirebase,
)(SignInFacebookBase);

const SignInTwitter = compose(
  withRouter,
  withFirebase,
)(SignInTwitterBase);

export default SignInPage;

export { SignInForm, SignInGoogle, SignInFacebook, SignInTwitter };
```

You will have an authenticated user afterward, but what's missing again is the database user that you have to create yourself:

src/components/SignIn/index.js

```
...

class SignInTwitterBase extends Component {
  ...

  onSubmit = event => {
    this.props.firebase
      .doSignInWithTwitter()
      .then(socialAuthUser => {
        // Create a user in your Firebase Realtime Database too
        return this.props.firebase
          .user(socialAuthUser.user.uid)
          .set({
            username: socialAuthUser.additionalUserInfo.profile.name,
            email: socialAuthUser.additionalUserInfo.profile.email,
            roles: {},
          });
      })
      .then(() => {
        this.setState({ error: null });
        this.props.history.push(ROUTES.HOME);
      })
      .catch(error => {
        this.setState({ error });
      });

    event.preventDefault();
  };

  ...
}

...
```

Again, every time a user signs in with Twitter, a new user with this stable id coming from the social login is created in your database. Basically if a user signs in twice with the same social login, the old user gets overridden. You can optionally make use of the socialuser.additionalUserInfo.isNewUser property to only create a new user when signing in with Twitter for the first time .

Exercises:

- Read more about the Twitter Social Login[80]
- Figure out whether there is a way to interact with Twitter's API afterward, because the `socialUser` has an `accessToken` and `secret` in its `credentials` object.
- Follow my Twitter[81] page to receive latest tutorials for web developers.
- Confirm your source code for the last section[82]

---

[80]https://firebase.google.com/docs/auth/web/twitter-login
[81]https://twitter.com/rwieruch
[82]http://bit.ly/2VuH8eh

Linking Social Logins to one Account

The last section walked you through implementing social logins for Google, Facebook, and Twitter to being able to sign up/in with a email/password combination. However, since you have enabled multiple accounts for one email address, there is more than one account associated to your email, which can lead to bugs for your service/product. Imagine a user signs in with Google, buys a ebook on your website, is able to download the book as signed in user, and then signs out again. The next sign-in with the email/password combination won't show the e-book anymore. This is because the user has two accounts on your website. While one account is associated with Google, the other one is associated with the email/password combination.

To walk through this scenario, take one of your social accounts (Google, Facebook, Twitter) and log into the Firebase in React application. Check the account page and copy the email address that is associated to your social account. Log out and log in again with your email/password combination, using the same email as for your social login. It's possible because we enabled multiple accounts for the same email address in the Firebase dashboard. When you check the account page again, you should see the same email as when you logged in with the social account. Now head to your Firebase dashboard and check the "Authentication" tab. You should find two accounts associated to the same email you used before. The same applies for the "Database" tab.

In this section, we want to prevent this behavior by using only one email address per user, while still being able to sign-in via email/password, Google, Facebook or Twitter. It shouldn't matter which sign-in you take, as the account should be the same. That's where the linking of all the social accounts comes in.

Before we get started, head to the Authentication and Database tabs on your Firebase dashboard and delete the user you used with your personal email address. We will use this email address later, except this time it will end up once in both tabs for one account. First, disable the setting on your Firebase dashboard that encourages email addresses associated to more than one account.

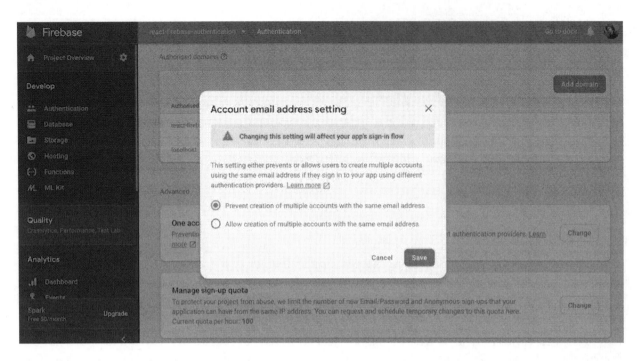

We will prevent the user from signing in with another account when there is already an account associated to this email address. A message should point the user to the account page to link all the social accounts and the email/password account with each other instead. Let's show the user a custom error message for the sign up page. First, extract the error code and the custom message as variables:

src/components/SignIn/index.js

```
const ERROR_CODE_ACCOUNT_EXISTS =
  'auth/account-exists-with-different-credential';

const ERROR_MSG_ACCOUNT_EXISTS = `
  An account with an E-Mail address to
  this social account already exists. Try to login from
  this account instead and associate your social accounts on
  your personal account page.
`;
```

Next, show the custom error message when the error code shows up. That's because we prevent more than one email address for one account:

src/components/SignIn/index.js

```
...

class SignInGoogleBase extends Component {
  ...

  onSubmit = event => {
    this.props.firebase
      .doSignInWithGoogle()
      .then(socialAuthUser => {
        ...
      })
      .then(() => {
        ...
      })
      .catch(error => {
        if (error.code === ERROR_CODE_ACCOUNT_EXISTS) {
          error.message = ERROR_MSG_ACCOUNT_EXISTS;
        }

        this.setState({ error });
      });

    event.preventDefault();
  };

  ...
}

...
```

Repeat this for the other social logins (Facebook, Twitter) as well. If a user signs in with one of the social logins, but there is already an account in the system with this email address, the custom error message shows up. The user has to log in with the correct sign-in method and link all other desired social accounts to this account on the account page. We will add this feature later in the account page, but before this, we need to show a similar custom error message for the sign up page as well. The user might use a social login first and later attempt to sign up with an email address (email/password sign up) that has been used by the social login already.

src/components/SignUp/index.js

```
const ERROR_CODE_ACCOUNT_EXISTS = 'auth/email-already-in-use';

const ERROR_MSG_ACCOUNT_EXISTS = `
  An account with this E-Mail address already exists.
  Try to login with this account instead. If you think the
  account is already used from one of the social logins, try
  to sign-in with one of them. Afterward, associate your accounts
  on your personal account page.
`;
```

Use the custom error message when the error code happens on sign-up:

src/components/SignUp/index.js

```
...

class SignUpFormBase extends Component {
  ...

  onSubmit = event => {
    const { username, email, passwordOne, isAdmin } = this.state;
    const roles = {};

    if (isAdmin) {
      roles[ROLES.ADMIN] = ROLES.ADMIN;
    }

    this.props.firebase
      .doCreateUserWithEmailAndPassword(email, passwordOne)
      .then(authUser => {
        ...
      })
      .then(() => {
        ...
      })
      .catch(error => {
        if (error.code === ERROR_CODE_ACCOUNT_EXISTS) {
          error.message = ERROR_MSG_ACCOUNT_EXISTS;
        }

        this.setState({ error });
      });
```

```
    event.preventDefault();
  };


  ...

}


...
```

Now users can use the same email address for different sign-in methods. Next, let's head to the account page, where we'll create an area to manage and activate/deactivate all the sign-in methods (social sign-ins, email/password sign-in). Introduce all available sign-in methods and their optional providers (see Firebase class) as list of objects:

src/components/Account/index.js

```
...

const SIGN_IN_METHODS = [
  {
    id: 'password',
    provider: null,
  },
  {
    id: 'google.com',
    provider: 'googleProvider',
  },
  {
    id: 'facebook.com',
    provider: 'facebookProvider',
  },
  {
    id: 'twitter.com',
    provider: 'twitterProvider',
  },
];

const AccountPage = () => (
  <AuthUserContext.Consumer>
    {authUser => (
      <div>
        <h1>Account: {authUser.email}</h1>
        <PasswordForgetForm />
        <PasswordChangeForm />
```

```
      <LoginManagement authUser={authUser} />
    </div>
  )}
  </AuthUserContext.Consumer>
);
```

. . .

Now implement the new component and render all available sign-in methods as buttons which are doing nothing:

src/components/Account/index.js

```
import React, { Component } from 'react';
```

. . .

```
class LoginManagement extends Component {
  render() {
    return (
      <div>
        Sign In Methods:
        <ul>
          {SIGN_IN_METHODS.map(signInMethod => {
            return (
              <li key={signInMethod.id}>
                <button type="button" onClick={() => {}}>
                  {signInMethod.id}
                </button>
              </li>
            );
          })}
        </ul>
      </div>
    );
  }
}
```

. . .

Remember to make the Firebase instance available to the component, because we need to use it in the next step:

src/components/Account/index.js

```
import React, { Component } from 'react';

import { AuthUserContext, withAuthorization } from '../Session';
import { withFirebase } from '../Firebase';
import { PasswordForgetForm } from '../PasswordForget';
import PasswordChangeForm from '../PasswordChange';

...

class LoginManagementBase extends Component {
  constructor(props) {
    ...
  }

  componentDidMount() {
    ...
  }

  render() {
    ...
  }
}

const LoginManagement = withFirebase(LoginManagementBase);

...
```

Then, fetch all active sign-in methods for the user's email address. Firebase has an API for it:

src/components/Account/index.js

```
...

class LoginManagementBase extends Component {
  constructor(props) {
    super(props);

    this.state = {
      activeSignInMethods: [],
      error: null,
    };
  }
```

```
componentDidMount() {
  this.props.firebase.auth
    .fetchSignInMethodsForEmail(this.props.authUser.email)
    .then(activeSignInMethods =>
      this.setState({ activeSignInMethods, error: null }),
    )
    .catch(error => this.setState({ error }));
}

  ...

}


...
```

Next, differentiate between active sign-in methods and the remaining sign-in methods not in the list of fetched sign-in methods. You can show an error message with a conditional rendering as well:

src/components/Account/index.js

```
class LoginManagementBase extends Component {
  ...

  render() {
    const { activeSignInMethods, error } = this.state;

    return (
      <div>
        Sign In Methods:
        <ul>
          {SIGN_IN_METHODS.map(signInMethod => {
            const isEnabled = activeSignInMethods.includes(
              signInMethod.id,
            );

            return (
              <li key={signInMethod.id}>
                {isEnabled ? (
                  <button type="button" onClick={() => {}}>
                    Deactivate {signInMethod.id}
                  </button>
                ) : (
                  <button type="button" onClick={() => {}}>
                    Link {signInMethod.id}
```

```
                </button>
              )}
          </li>
        );
      })}
    </ul>
    {error && error.message}
  </div>
);
  }
}
```

While all available sign-in methods are displayed, they differentiate between active and non-active. The active methods can be deactivated. On the other hand, sign-in methods that are available but not used by the user can be linked instead to make them active. We will implement both details in the next step:

src/components/Account/index.js

```
class LoginManagementBase extends Component {
  ...

  componentDidMount() {
    this.fetchSignInMethods();
  }

  fetchSignInMethods = () => {
    this.props.firebase.auth
      .fetchSignInMethodsForEmail(this.props.authUser.email)
      .then(activeSignInMethods =>
        this.setState({ activeSignInMethods, error: null }),
      )
      .catch(error => this.setState({ error }));
  };

  onSocialLoginLink = provider => {
    ...
  };

  onUnlink = providerId => {
    ...
  };
```

```
  ...
}
```

Extract the fetch method, because we will use it after we linked (activated) or unlinked (deactivated) sign-in methods. Then the new class methods can be used by the buttons:

src/components/Account/index.js

```
class LoginManagementBase extends Component {
  ...

  render() {
    const { activeSignInMethods, error } = this.state;

    return (
      <div>
        Sign In Methods:
        <ul>
          {SIGN_IN_METHODS.map(signInMethod => {
            const onlyOneLeft = activeSignInMethods.length === 1;
            const isEnabled = activeSignInMethods.includes(
              signInMethod.id,
            );

            return (
              <li key={signInMethod.id}>
                {isEnabled ? (
                  <button
                    type="button"
                    onClick={() => this.onUnlink(signInMethod.id)}
                    disabled={onlyOneLeft}
                  >
                    Deactivate {signInMethod.id}
                  </button>
                ) : (
                  <button
                    type="button"
                    onClick={() =>
                      this.onSocialLoginLink(signInMethod.provider)
                    }
                  >
                    Link {signInMethod.id}
                  </button>
                )}
```

```
        </li>
      );
    })}
  </ul>
  {error && error.message}
</div>
    );
  }
}
```

Also, we added an improvement to avoid getting locked out of the application. If only one sign-in method is left as active, disable all deactivation buttons because there needs to be at least one sign-in method. Now let's implement the class methods for linking and unlinking accounts:

src/components/Account/index.js

```
class LoginManagementBase extends Component {
  ...

  onSocialLoginLink = provider => {
    this.props.firebase.auth.currentUser
      .linkWithPopup(this.props.firebase[provider])
      .then(this.fetchSignInMethods)
      .catch(error => this.setState({ error }));
  };

  onUnlink = providerId => {
    this.props.firebase.auth.currentUser
      .unlink(providerId)
      .then(this.fetchSignInMethods)
      .catch(error => this.setState({ error }));
  };

  ...
}
```

Finally we are able to link and unlink accounts. Afterward, all active sign-in methods are fetched again. That's why we have extracted this class method from the componentDidMount() lifecycle method before, which is reusable now. The linking of the sign-in methods should work for Google, Facebook and Twitter now. However, it doesn't work for the email/password combination yet, because this one isn't done by a simple button click. If the user has only active social sign-in methods but no email/password sign-in method, an email/password combination must be provided; then it is possible to link this sign-in method to the other social sign-in methods.

First, extract the social sign-in methods to its own component and add a conditional rendering for the password sign-in method:

src/components/Account/index.js

```
class LoginManagementBase extends Component {
  ...

  onDefaultLoginLink = () => {
    ...
  };

  render() {
    const { activeSignInMethods, error } = this.state;

    return (
      <div>
        Sign In Methods:
        <ul>
          {SIGN_IN_METHODS.map(signInMethod => {

            ...

            return (
              <li key={signInMethod.id}>
                {signInMethod.id === 'password' ? (
                  <DefaultLoginToggle
                    onlyOneLeft={onlyOneLeft}
                    isEnabled={isEnabled}
                    signInMethod={signInMethod}
                    onLink={this.onDefaultLoginLink}
                    onUnlink={this.onUnlink}
                  />
                ) : (
                  <SocialLoginToggle
                    onlyOneLeft={onlyOneLeft}
                    isEnabled={isEnabled}
                    signInMethod={signInMethod}
                    onLink={this.onSocialLoginLink}
                    onUnlink={this.onUnlink}
                  />
                )}
              </li>
            );
          })}
```

```
      </ul>
      {error && error.message}
    </div>
  );
  }
}
```

The DefaultLoginToggle component will use a different onLink handler than the SocialLoginToggle component, but the onUnlink stays the same. We will implement DefaultLoginToggle component and its missing handler in a moment, but first let's extract the SocialLoginToggle component:

src/components/Account/index.js

```
const SocialLoginToggle = ({
  onlyOneLeft,
  isEnabled,
  signInMethod,
  onLink,
  onUnlink,
}) =>
  isEnabled ? (
    <button
      type="button"
      onClick={() => onUnlink(signInMethod.id)}
      disabled={onlyOneLeft}
    >
      Deactivate {signInMethod.id}
    </button>
  ) : (
    <button
      type="button"
      onClick={() => onLink(signInMethod.provider)}
    >
      Link {signInMethod.id}
    </button>
  );
```

The implementation details didn't change, but the component is standalone now. Next, let's implement the other component for the email/password sign-in. When this sign-in method is activated, it's sufficient to render only a button similar to the social sign-in methods to unlink (deactivate) this sign-in method. If this sign-in method isn't activated, you need to retrieve the user's desired email and password combination to link it as account to the other social accounts. It's very similar to our sign up form then:

src/components/Account/index.js

```javascript
class DefaultLoginToggle extends Component {
  constructor(props) {
    super(props);

    this.state = { passwordOne: '', passwordTwo: '' };
  }

  onSubmit = event => {
    event.preventDefault();

    this.props.onLink(this.state.passwordOne);
    this.setState({ passwordOne: '', passwordTwo: '' });
  };

  onChange = event => {
    this.setState({ [event.target.name]: event.target.value });
  };

  render() {
    const {
      onlyOneLeft,
      isEnabled,
      signInMethod,
      onUnlink,
    } = this.props;

    const { passwordOne, passwordTwo } = this.state;

    const isInvalid =
      passwordOne !== passwordTwo || passwordOne === '';

    return isEnabled ? (
      <button
        type="button"
        onClick={() => onUnlink(signInMethod.id)}
        disabled={onlyOneLeft}
      >
        Deactivate {signInMethod.id}
      </button>
    ) : (
      <form onSubmit={this.onSubmit}>
        <input
```

```
        name="passwordOne"
        value={passwordOne}
        onChange={this.onChange}
        type="password"
        placeholder="New Password"
      />
      <input
        name="passwordTwo"
        value={passwordTwo}
        onChange={this.onChange}
        type="password"
        placeholder="Confirm New Password"
      />

      <button disabled={isInvalid} type="submit">
        Link {signInMethod.id}
      </button>
    </form>
  );
  }
}
```

Next, let's implement the handler in the parent component for the default sign-in via email/password. It receives a password from the child component, which is added to the authenticated user's email address:

src/components/Account/index.js

```
class LoginManagementBase extends Component {
  ...

  onDefaultLoginLink = password => {
    const credential = this.props.firebase.emailAuthProvider.credential(
      this.props.authUser.email,
      password,
    );

    this.props.firebase.auth.currentUser
      .linkAndRetrieveDataWithCredential(credential)
      .then(this.fetchSignInMethods)
      .catch(error => this.setState({ error }));
  };
```

```
    . . .
}
```

The Firebase API is not too elegant here, but it's good to know that it creates a credential from the user's email and desired password. Afterward, it links it to the other accounts. Then all active sign-in methods are fetched again to keep everything updated.

Previously, when we set up our Firebase class, we overrode its auth property with app.auth(). However, to create the credential from the email and password in the component, we need access to the Firebase internal auth, which has the EmailAuthProvider property, so we reference it before we override it with app.auth() in the next lines.

src/components/Firebase/firebase.js

```
. . .

class Firebase {
  constructor() {
    app.initializeApp(config);

    this.emailAuthProvider = app.auth.EmailAuthProvider;
    this.auth = app.auth();
    this.db = app.database();

    this.googleProvider = new app.auth.GoogleAuthProvider();
    this.facebookProvider = new app.auth.FacebookAuthProvider();
    this.twitterProvider = new app.auth.TwitterAuthProvider();
  }

  . . .
}

. . .
```

Now you can link and unlink different sign-in methods using only one account and email address.

Exercises:

- Try to link and unlink different sign-in methods and check if you are able to sign-in with this method afterwards.
- Implement loading indicators for each button that activate and deactivate the sign-in methods for a better user experience.

- Read more about social account linking in Firebase[83]
- Confirm your source code for the last section[84]

---

[83]https://firebase.google.com/docs/auth/web/account-linking
[84]http://bit.ly/2VnF3Rf

Email Verification

In your application, users can employ an email/password combination, but also social logins to get access to your service or product. Often, the email address associated with the social logins is confirmed by the social platform (Google, Facebook, Twitter) and you know this email address really exists. But what about the email address used with the password? Because users are sometimes unwilling to provide real email addresses, they'll simply make one up, so you can't provide them with further information via email or to integrate them with third-parties where a valid email address is required. In this section, I will show you how to confirm user email addresses before they can access your application. After an email verification with a double opt-in send by email, users are authorized to use your application.

Because the Firebase API already provides this functionality, we can add it to our Firebase class to make it available for our React application. Provide an optional redirect URL that is used to navigate to the application after email confirmation:

src/components/Firebase/firebase.js

```
...

class Firebase {
  ...

  // *** Auth API ***

  ...

  doSendEmailVerification = () =>
    this.auth.currentUser.sendEmailVerification({
      url: process.env.REACT_APP_CONFIRMATION_EMAIL_REDIRECT,
    });

  ...
}

export default Firebase;
```

You can inline this URL, but also put it into your *.env* file(s). I prefer environment variables for development (*.env.development*) and production (*.env.production*). The development environment receives the localhost URL:

.env.development

```
. . .
```

```
REACT_APP_CONFIRMATION_EMAIL_REDIRECT=http://localhost:3000
```

And the production environment receives an actual domain:

.env.production

```
. . .
```

```
REACT_APP_CONFIRMATION_EMAIL_REDIRECT=https://mydomain.com
```

That's all we need to do for the API. The best place to guide users through the email verification is during email and password sign-up:

src/components/SignUp/index.js

```
. . .

class SignUpFormBase extends Component {
  . . .

  onSubmit = event => {
    . . .

    this.props.firebase
      .doCreateUserWithEmailAndPassword(email, passwordOne)
      .then(authUser => {
        // Create a user in your Firebase realtime database
        return this.props.firebase.user(authUser.user.uid).set({
          username,
          email,
          roles,
        });
      })
      .then(() => {
        return this.props.firebase.doSendEmailVerification();
      })
      .then(() => {
        this.setState({ ...INITIAL_STATE });
        this.props.history.push(ROUTES.HOME);
      })
```

```
        .catch(error => {
          ...
        });

    event.preventDefault();
  };


  ...
}
```

...

Users will receive a verification email when they register for your application. To find out if a user has a verified email, you can retrieve this information from the authenticated user in your Firebase class:

src/components/Firebase/firebase.js

```
...

class Firebase {
  ...

  // *** Merge Auth and DB User API *** //

  onAuthUserListener = (next, fallback) =>
    this.auth.onAuthStateChanged(authUser => {
      if (authUser) {
        this.user(authUser.uid)
          .once('value')
          .then(snapshot => {
            const dbUser = snapshot.val();

            // default empty roles
            if (!dbUser.roles) {
              dbUser.roles = {};
            }

            // merge auth and db user
            authUser = {
              uid: authUser.uid,
              email: authUser.email,
              emailVerified: authUser.emailVerified,
              providerData: authUser.providerData,
```

```
            ...dbUser,
          };

          next(authUser);
        });
    } else {
      fallback();
    }
  });

  ...
}
```

```
export default Firebase;
```

To protect your routes from users who have no verified email address, we will do it with a new higher-order component in *src/components/Session/withEmailVerification.js* that has access to Firebase and the authenticated user:

src/components/Session/withEmailVerification.js

```
import React from 'react';

import AuthUserContext from './context';
import { withFirebase } from '../Firebase';

const withEmailVerification = Component => {
  class WithEmailVerification extends React.Component {
    render() {
      return (
        <AuthUserContext.Consumer>
          {authUser => <Component {...this.props} />}
        </AuthUserContext.Consumer>
      );
    }
  }

  return withFirebase(WithEmailVerification);
};

export default withEmailVerification;
```

Add a function in this file that checks if the authenticated user has a verified email and an email/password sign in on associated with it. If the user has only social logins, it doesn't matter if the email is not verified.

src/components/Session/withEmailVerification.js

```
const needsEmailVerification = authUser =>
  authUser &&
  !authUser.emailVerified &&
  authUser.providerData
    .map(provider => provider.providerId)
    .includes('password');
```

If this is true, don't render the component passed to this higher-order component, but a message that reminds users to verify their email addresses.

src/components/Session/withEmailVerification.js

```
...

const withEmailVerification = Component => {
  class WithEmailVerification extends React.Component {
    onSendEmailVerification = () => {
      this.props.firebase.doSendEmailVerification();
    }

    render() {
      return (
        <AuthUserContext.Consumer>
          {authUser =>
            needsEmailVerification(authUser) ? (
              <div>
                <p>
                  Verify your E-Mail: Check you E-Mails (Spam folder
                  included) for a confirmation E-Mail or send
                  another confirmation E-Mail.
                </p>

                <button
                  type="button"
                  onClick={this.onSendEmailVerification}
                >
                  Send confirmation E-Mail
                </button>
              </div>
            ) : (
```

```
            <Component {...this.props} />
          )
        }
      </AuthUserContext.Consumer>
    );
  }
}

  return withFirebase(WithEmailVerification);
};


export default withEmailVerification;
```

Optionally, we can provide a button to resend a verification email to the user. Let's improve the user experience. After the button is clicked to resend the verification email, users should receive feedback, and be prohibited from sending another email. First, add a local state to the higher-order component that tracks whether the button was clicked:

src/components/Session/withEmailVerification.js

```
...

const withEmailVerification = Component => {
  class WithEmailVerification extends React.Component {
    constructor(props) {
      super(props);

      this.state = { isSent: false };
    }

    onSendEmailVerification = () => {
      this.props.firebase
        .doSendEmailVerification()
        .then(() => this.setState({ isSent: true }));
    };


    ...

  }

  return withFirebase(WithEmailVerification);
};


export default withEmailVerification;
```

Second, show another message with a conditional rendering if a user has sent another verification email:

src/components/Session/withEmailVerification.js

```
...

const withEmailVerification = Component => {
  class WithEmailVerification extends React.Component {

    ...

    render() {
      return (
        <AuthUserContext.Consumer>
          {authUser =>
            needsEmailVerification(authUser) ? (
              <div>
                {this.state.isSent ? (
                  <p>
                    E-Mail confirmation sent: Check you E-Mails (Spam
                    folder included) for a confirmation E-Mail.
                    Refresh this page once you confirmed your E-Mail.
                  </p>
                ) : (
                  <p>
                    Verify your E-Mail: Check you E-Mails (Spam folder
                    included) for a confirmation E-Mail or send
                    another confirmation E-Mail.
                  </p>
                )}

                <button
                  type="button"
                  onClick={this.onSendEmailVerification}
                  disabled={this.state.isSent}
                >
                  Send confirmation E-Mail
                </button>
              </div>
            ) : (
              <Component {...this.props} />
            )
          }
```

```
        </AuthUserContext.Consumer>
      );
    }
  }

  return withFirebase(WithEmailVerification);
};


export default withEmailVerification;
```

Lastly, make the new higher-order component available in your Session folder's *index.js* file:

src/components/Session/index.js

```
import AuthUserContext from './context';
import withAuthentication from './withAuthentication';
import withAuthorization from './withAuthorization';
import withEmailVerification from './withEmailVerification';

export {
  AuthUserContext,
  withAuthentication,
  withAuthorization,
  withEmailVerification,
};
```

Send a confirmation email once a user signs up with a email/password combination. You also have a higher-order component used for authorization and optionally resending a confirmation email. Next, secure all pages/routes that should be only accessible with a confirmed email. Let's begin with the home page:

src/components/Home/index.js

```
import React from 'react';
import { compose } from 'recompose';

import { withAuthorization, withEmailVerification } from '../Session';

const HomePage = () => (
  <div>
    <h1>Home Page</h1>
    <p>The Home Page is accessible by every signed in user.</p>
  </div>
);
```

```
const condition = authUser => !!authUser;

export default compose(
  withEmailVerification,
  withAuthorization(condition),
)(HomePage);
```

Next the admin page:

src/components/Admin/index.js

```
import React, { Component } from 'react';
import { compose } from 'recompose';

import { withFirebase } from '../Firebase';
import { withAuthorization, withEmailVerification } from '../Session';
import * as ROLES from '../../constants/roles';

...

const condition = authUser =>
  authUser && !!authUser.roles[ROLES.ADMIN];

export default compose(
  withEmailVerification,
  withAuthorization(condition),
  withFirebase,
)(AdminPage);
```

And the account page:

src/components/Account/index.js

```
import React, { Component } from 'react';
import { compose } from 'recompose';

import {
  AuthUserContext,
  withAuthorization,
  withEmailVerification,
} from '../Session';
import { withFirebase } from '../Firebase';
import { PasswordForgetForm } from '../PasswordForget';
```

```
import PasswordChangeForm from '../PasswordChange';

...

const condition = authUser => !!authUser;

export default compose(
  withEmailVerification,
  withAuthorization(condition),
)(AccountPage);
```

All the sensible routes for authenticated users now require a confirmed email. Finally, your application can be only used by users with real email addresses.

Exercises:

- Familiarize yourself with the new flow by deleting your user from the Authentication and Realtime Databases and sign up again.
  - For example, sign up with a social login instead of the email/password combination, but activate the email/password sign in method later on the account page.
  - This is in general a good way to purge the database to start from a clean slate if anything feels buggy.
- Implement the "Send confirmation E-Mail" button in a way that it's not shown the first time a user signs up; otherwise the user may be tempted to click the button right away and receives a second confirmation E-Mail.
- Read more about Firebase's verification E-Mail[85]
- Read more about additional configuration for the verification E-Mail[86]
- Confirm your source code for the last section[87]

---

[85]https://firebase.google.com/docs/auth/web/manage-users
[86]https://firebase.google.com/docs/auth/web/passing-state-in-email-actions
[87]http://bit.ly/2Vqtfxt

Admin Dashboard

Before we dive deeper into Firebase's realtime database and the domain-related business logic of our application, it makes sense to invest more time into React Router. So far, we have split up our application into top-level routes to manage our whole authentication flow with login, logout, and registration. Additionally, we protected top-level routes with authorization that checks for authenticated users, confirmed email addresses, and admin users.

In this section, we'll implement more specific routing for the admin page. So far, this page only shows a list of users, retrieved from the Firebase realtime database. Basically, it is the overview of our users. However, a list of users alone doesn't help that much, and a detail page would be much more useful. Then, it would be possible to trigger further actions for the user on the detail page instead of the overview page. To start, define a new child route:

src/constants/routes.js

```
export const LANDING = '/';
export const SIGN_UP = '/signup';
export const SIGN_IN = '/signin';
export const HOME = '/home';
export const ACCOUNT = '/account';
export const PASSWORD_FORGET = '/pw-forget';
export const ADMIN = '/admin';
export const ADMIN_DETAILS = '/admin/:id';
```

The :id is a placeholder for a user identifier to be used later. If you want to be more specific, you could have used /admin/users/:id as well. Perhaps later you'll want to manage other entities on this admin page. For instance, the admin page could have a list of users and a list of books written by them, where it would make sense to have detail pages for users (/admin/users/:userId) and books (/admin/books/:bookId).

Next, extract all the functionality from the AdminPage component. You will lift this business logic down to another component in the next step. In this step, introduce two sub routes for the admin page and match the UserList and UserItem components to it. The former component is already there, the latter component will be implemented soon.

src/components/Admin/index.js

```
import React, { Component } from 'react';
import { Switch, Route, Link } from 'react-router-dom';
import { compose } from 'recompose';

import { withFirebase } from '../Firebase';
import { withAuthorization, withEmailVerification } from '../Session';
import * as ROLES from '../../constants/roles';
import * as ROUTES from '../../constants/routes';

const AdminPage = () => (
  <div>
    <h1>Admin</h1>
    <p>The Admin Page is accessible by every signed in admin user.</p>

    <Switch>
      <Route exact path={ROUTES.ADMIN_DETAILS} component={UserItem} />
      <Route exact path={ROUTES.ADMIN} component={UserList} />
    </Switch>
  </div>
);
```

The UserList component receives all the business logic that was in the AdminPage. Also, it receives the Base suffix because we enhance it in the next step with a higher-order component to make the Firebase instance available.

src/components/Admin/index.js

```
class UserListBase extends Component {
  constructor(props) {
    super(props);

    this.state = {
      loading: false,
      users: [],
    };
  }

  componentDidMount() {
    this.setState({ loading: true });

    this.props.firebase.users().on('value', snapshot => {
      const usersObject = snapshot.val();
```

```
      const usersList = Object.keys(usersObject).map(key => ({
        ...usersObject[key],
        uid: key,
      }));

      this.setState({
        users: usersList,
        loading: false,
      });
    });
  }

  componentWillUnmount() {
    this.props.firebase.users().off();
  }

  render() {
    ...
  }
}
```

Further, the UserList component renders a Link component from the React Router package, which is used to navigate users from the user list (overview) to the user item (detail) route. The mapping for the route and the component was completed in the AdminPage component.

src/components/Admin/index.js

```
class UserListBase extends Component {
  ...

  render() {
    const { users, loading } = this.state;

    return (
      <div>
        <h2>Users</h2>
        {loading && <div>Loading ...</div>}
        <ul>
          {users.map(user => (
            <li key={user.uid}>
              <span>
                <strong>ID:</strong> {user.uid}
              </span>
```

```
            <span>
              <strong>E-Mail:</strong> {user.email}
            </span>
            <span>
              <strong>Username:</strong> {user.username}
            </span>
            <span>
              <Link to={`${ROUTES.ADMIN}/${user.uid}`}>
                Details
              </Link>
            </span>
          </li>
        ))}
      </ul>
    </div>
  );
 }
}
```

Remember, the UserList receives access to the Firebase instance, and the AdminPage doesn't need it anymore.

src/components/Admin/index.js

```
...

const condition = authUser =>
  authUser && !!authUser.roles[ROLES.ADMIN];

const UserList = withFirebase(UserListBase);

export default compose(
  withEmailVerification,
  withAuthorization(condition),
)(AdminPage);
```

Last but not least, render a basic UserItem component.

src/components/Admin/index.js

```
...

const UserItem = ({ match }) => (
  <div>
    <h2>User ({match.params.id})</h2>
  </div>
);
```

You should be able to navigate from the user list (overview) to the user item (detail) component on the admin page now. We are fetching the user list on the admin page, without specific user data for a single user for the UserItem component on the detail perspective. The identifier for the user is available from the browser's URL through the React Router. You can extract it from the component's props to fetch a user from Firebase's realtime database:

src/components/Admin/index.js

```
class UserItemBase extends Component {
  constructor(props) {
    super(props);

    this.state = {
      loading: false,
      user: null,
    };
  }

  componentDidMount() {
    this.setState({ loading: true });

    this.props.firebase
      .user(this.props.match.params.id)
      .on('value', snapshot => {
        this.setState({
          user: snapshot.val(),
          loading: false,
        });
      });
  }

  componentWillUnmount() {
    this.props.firebase.user(this.props.match.params.id).off();
  }
```

```
  render() {
    ...
  }
}
```

Don't forget to make Firebase accessible in the props of the UserItem component again via our higher-order component:

src/components/Admin/index.js

```
...


const UserList = withFirebase(UserListBase);
const UserItem = withFirebase(UserItemBase);


...
```

Last but not least, render again the user information. This time it's not a whole list of users, but only a single user entity:

src/components/Admin/index.js

```
class UserItemBase extends Component {
  ...

  render() {
    const { user, loading } = this.state;

    return (
      <div>
        <h2>User ({this.props.match.params.id})</h2>
        {loading && <div>Loading ...</div>}

        {user && (
          <div>
            <span>
              <strong>ID:</strong> {user.uid}
            </span>
            <span>
              <strong>E-Mail:</strong> {user.email}
            </span>
            <span>
              <strong>Username:</strong> {user.username}
```

```
        </span>
      </div>
    )}
    </div>
  );
  }
}
```

When you navigate to a user detail perspective, you can see the id from the props is rendered immediately, because it's available from React Router to fetch user details from the Firebase database. However, since you already have the information about the user in the UserList component that links to your UserItem component, you can pass this information through React Router's Link:

src/components/Admin/index.js

```
class UserListBase extends Component {
  ...

  render() {
    const { users, loading } = this.state;

    return (
      <div>
        <h2>Users</h2>
        {loading && <div>Loading ...</div>}
        <ul>
          {users.map(user => (
            <li key={user.uid}>
              ...
              <span>
                <Link
                  to={{
                    pathname: `${ROUTES.ADMIN}/${user.uid}`,
                    state: { user },
                  }}
                >
                  Details
                </Link>
              </span>
            </li>
          ))}
        </ul>
      </div>
    );
```

```
  }
}
```

Then use it in the UserItem component as default local state:

src/components/Admin/index.js

```
class UserItemBase extends Component {
  constructor(props) {
    super(props);

    this.state = {
      loading: false,
      user: null,
      ...props.location.state,
    };
  }

  componentDidMount() {
    if (this.state.user) {
      return;
    }

    this.setState({ loading: true });

    this.props.firebase
      .user(this.props.match.params.id)
      .on('value', snapshot => {
        this.setState({
          user: snapshot.val(),
          loading: false,
        });
      });
  }

  ...

}
```

If users navigate from the UserList to the UserItem component, they should arrive immediately. If they enter the URL by hand in the browser or with a Link component that doesn't pass them to the UserItem component, the user needs to be fetched from the Firebase database. Since you have a page for each individual user on your admin dashboard now, you can add more specific actions. For instance, sometimes a user can't login and isn't sure how to proceed, which is the perfect time to send a reset password email to them as admin. Let's add a button to send a password reset email to a user.

src/components/Admin/index.js

```
class UserItemBase extends Component {
  ...

  onSendPasswordResetEmail = () => {
    this.props.firebase.doPasswordReset(this.state.user.email);
  };

  render() {
    const { user, loading } = this.state;

    return (
      <div>
        <h2>User ({this.props.match.params.id})</h2>
        {loading && <div>Loading ...</div>}

        {user && (
          <div>
            ...
            <span>
              <strong>Username:</strong> {user.username}
            </span>
            <span>
              <button
                type="button"
                onClick={this.onSendPasswordResetEmail}
              >
                Send Password Reset
              </button>
            </span>
          </div>
        )}
      </div>
    );
  }
}
```

Note: If you want to dig deeper into deleting users from Firebase's authentication, how to resend verification emails, or how to change email addresses, study Firebase's Admin SDK.

This section has shown you how to implement more specific routes with React Router and how to interact with the Firebase database on each individual route. You can also use React Router's advanced features to pass information as props to the other components like we did for the user.

Exercises:

- Learn more about React Router[88]
- Read more about Firebase's Admin SDK[89]
- Confirm your source code for the last section[90]

---

[88]https://reacttraining.com/react-router/web/guides/quick-start
[89]https://firebase.google.com/docs/auth/admin/
[90]http://bit.ly/2VnfIqw

Firebase Realtime Database (2): Advanced

Now we've worked with a list of data and single entities with the Firebase's realtime database to create an admin dashboard in the previous sections. In this section, I want to introduce a new entity to demonstrate a business-related feature for a Firebase in React application, a message entity that lets you create a chat application. We'll cover how to interact with Firebase's realtime database; specifically, how to structure data, work with lists of data, and how to create, update, and remove data. Also, you will see how ordering and pagination works with Firebase. In the end, it's up to you to decide whether your application should become a chat application with a message entity or a book application with a book entity in the database. The message entity is only there as example.

Defining the API

Our Firebase class is the glue between our React application and the Firebase API. We instantiate it once, and then pass it to our React application via React's Context API. Then, we can define all APIs to connect both worlds in the Firebase class. We completed it earlier for the authentication API and the user management. Next, let's introduce the API for the new message entity.

src/components/Firebase/firebase.js

```
class Firebase {

  ...

  // *** User API ***

  user = uid => this.db.ref(`users/${uid}`);

  users = () => this.db.ref('users');

  // *** Message API ***

  message = uid => this.db.ref(`messages/${uid}`);

  messages = () => this.db.ref('messages');
}
```

Messages are readable and writeable on two API endpoints: messages and messages/:messageId. You will retrieve a list of messages and create a message with the messages reference, but you will edit and remove messages with the messages/:messageId reference.

If you want to be more specific, put more informative class methods for the message API in your Firebase class. For instance, there could be one class method for creating, updating, and removing a message. We will keep it general, however, and perform the specifics in the React components.

How to fetch a List

The HomePage component might be the best place to add the chat feature with messages, which is only accessible by authenticated users due to authorization. Let's add a Message component that has access to the Firebase instance:

src/components/Home/index.js

```javascript
import React, { Component } from 'react';
import { compose } from 'recompose';

import { withAuthorization, withEmailVerification } from '../Session';
import { withFirebase } from '../Firebase';

const HomePage = () => (
  <div>
    <h1>Home Page</h1>
    <p>The Home Page is accessible by every signed in user.</p>

    <Messages />
  </div>
);

class MessagesBase extends Component {
  ...
}

const Messages = withFirebase(MessagesBase);

export default compose(
  withEmailVerification,
  withAuthorization(condition),
)(HomePage);
```

The Messages component has a local state for a loading indicator and the list of messages. In the lifecycle methods of the component, you can initialize (and remove) listeners to get messages from the Firebase database in realtime. When messages change (create, update, remove), the callback function in the listener is triggered and Firebase provides a snapshot of the data.

src/components/Home/index.js

```
class MessagesBase extends Component {
  constructor(props) {
    super(props);

    this.state = {
      loading: false,
      messages: [],
    };
  }

  componentDidMount() {
    this.setState({ loading: true });

    this.props.firebase.messages().on('value', snapshot => {
      // convert messages list from snapshot

      this.setState({ loading: false });
    });
  }

  componentWillUnmount() {
    this.props.firebase.messages().off();
  }

  render() {
    const { messages, loading } = this.state;

    return (
      <div>
        {loading && <div>Loading ...</div>}

        <MessageList messages={messages} />
      </div>
    );
  }
}
```

The new MessageList and MessageItem components only render the message content:

src/components/Home/index.js

```
const MessageList = ({ messages }) => (
  <ul>
    {messages.map(message => (
      <MessageItem key={message.uid} message={message} />
    ))}
  </ul>
);

const MessageItem = ({ message }) => (
  <li>
    <strong>{message.userId}</strong> {message.text}
  </li>
);
```

If you run the application, the loading indicator disappears after a few seconds when the Firebase realtime database listener is called for the first time. Every other time the loading indicator isn't shown, because it is only true when the component mounts and the first message fetching starts.

It could be that there are no messages yet, which is the case for this application since we didn't use the message API to create a message yet. We're only showing the messages for now. To show conditional feedback to users, we need to know if the list of messages is empty (see constructor), if the message API didn't return any messages and the local state is changed from an empty array to null:

src/components/Home/index.js

```
class MessagesBase extends Component {
  constructor(props) {
    super(props);

    this.state = {
      loading: false,
      messages: [],
    };
  }

  componentDidMount() {
    this.setState({ loading: true });

    this.props.firebase.messages().on('value', snapshot => {
      const messageObject = snapshot.val();

      if (messageObject) {
```

```
      // convert messages list from snapshot

      this.setState({ loading: false });
    } else {
      this.setState({ messages: null, loading: false });
    }
  });
}

...

render() {
  const { messages, loading } = this.state;

  return (
    <div>
      {loading && <div>Loading ...</div>}

      {messages ? (
        <MessageList messages={messages} />
      ) : (
        <div>There are no messages ...</div>
      )}
    </div>
  );
}
}
```

Lastly, you need to convert the messages from the snapshot object to a list of items. Since Firebase comes with its own internal representation of data, you need to transform the data as before for the list of users on the admin page:

src/components/Home/index.js

```
class MessagesBase extends Component {
  ...

  componentDidMount() {
    this.setState({ loading: true });

    this.props.firebase.messages().on('value', snapshot => {
      const messageObject = snapshot.val();

      if (messageObject) {
```

```
      const messageList = Object.keys(messageObject).map(key => ({
        ...messageObject[key],
        uid: key,
      }));

      this.setState({
        messages: messageList,
        loading: false,
      });
    } else {
      this.setState({ messages: null, loading: false });
    }
  });
}

  ...
}
```

Since you have no messages, nothing shows up. Creating chat messages is our next task.

Creating an Item in a List

We were able to get all messages from the Firebase realtime database. It's even updated for us using the Firebase listener on a reference with the on and not once method. Next, let's implement a React form that lets us create a message entity in the Firebase realtime database:

src/components/Home/index.js

```
class MessagesBase extends Component {
  ...

  render() {
    const { text, messages, loading } = this.state;

    return (
      <div>
        {loading && <div>Loading ...</div>}

        {messages ? (
          <MessageList messages={messages} />
        ) : (
          <div>There are no messages ...</div>
        )}

        <form onSubmit={this.onCreateMessage}>
          <input
            type="text"
            value={text}
            onChange={this.onChangeText}
          />
          <button type="submit">Send</button>
        </form>
      </div>
    );
  }
}
```

Next, add the new initial state for the component to keep track of the text property for a new message and its two new class methods to update the text in an input field element and create the actual message with Firebase:

src/components/Home/index.js

```
class MessagesBase extends Component {
  constructor(props) {
    super(props);

    this.state = {
      text: '',
      loading: false,
      messages: [],
    };
  }

  ...

  onChangeText = event => {
    this.setState({ text: event.target.value });
  };

  onCreateMessage = event => {
    this.props.firebase.messages().push({
      text: this.state.text,
    });

    this.setState({ text: '' });

    event.preventDefault();
  };

  ...
}
```

We can use the push method on a Firebase reference to create a new entity in this list of entities, though we don't want to create a message just yet. One piece is missing for associating messages to users, which needs to be implemented before we create messages.

Relationships

If you look closer at the MessageItem component, you can see that a message not only has a text, but also a userId that can be used to associate the message to a user. Let's use the authenticated user from our React Context to store the user identifier in a new message. First, add the Consumer component and add the identifier for the authenticated user in the class method call that creates the message:

src/components/Home/index.js

```
...

import {
  AuthUserContext,
  withAuthorization,
  withEmailVerification,
} from '../Session';

...

class MessagesBase extends Component {
  ...

  render() {
    const { text, messages, loading } = this.state;

    return (
      <AuthUserContext.Consumer>
        {authUser => (
          <div>
            {loading && <div>Loading ...</div>}

            {messages ? (
              <MessageList messages={messages} />
            ) : (
              <div>There are no messages ...</div>
            )}

            <form onSubmit={event => this.onCreateMessage(event, authUser)}>
              <input
                type="text"
                value={text}
                onChange={this.onChangeText}
```

```
          />
          <button type="submit">Send</button>
        </form>
      </div>
    )}
  </AuthUserContext.Consumer>
 );
 }
}
```

Next, use the authenticated user to associate the user identifier to the message. It makes sense to use the authenticated user, because this is the person authorized to write messages:

src/components/Home/index.js

```
class MessagesBase extends Component {
  ...

  onCreateMessage = (event, authUser) => {
    this.props.firebase.messages().push({
      text: this.state.text,
      userId: authUser.uid,
    });

    this.setState({ text: '' });

    event.preventDefault();
  };


  ...
}
```

Now go ahead and create a message. Since we only can access this page as an authenticated user due to authorization, we know that each message that is written here will be associated to a user identifier. After you have created a message, the realtime feature of the Firebase database makes sure that the message will show up in our rendered list.

So far, we have chosen to keep the footprint of a user entity within a message as little as possible. There is only an user identifier which associates the message to a user. Generally speaking it's good to structure data in your database this way, because it avoids plenty of pitfalls. For instance, let's imagine you would associate the whole user entity to a message and not only the identifier. Then every time a user entity changes in the database, you would have to change the message entity with the user as well. That's a common problem when not following the principal of the single source of truth when designing your database models. In our case, we are associating entities with each other only by their identifiers instead, whereas each entity in the database is the single source of truth without any duplications.

Another thing we decided earlier is giving the messages their dedicated API reference with `messages`. In another scenario, it could have been `users/:userId/messages` to associate users directly with the message via the reference. But doing it this way, we would have to fetch messages from multiple API endpoints in the end to show a nice chatroom as we do it right now.

Removing an Item in a List

We are reading a list of messages and created our first message. What about the other two missing functionalities to remove and edit a message. Let's continue with removing a message. Pass through a new class method that will remove a message eventually:

src/components/Home/index.js

```
class MessagesBase extends Component {
  ...

  onRemoveMessage = () => {
    ...
  };

  render() {
    const { text, messages, loading } = this.state;

    return (
      <AuthUserContext.Consumer>
        {authUser => (
          <div>

            ...

            {messages ? (
              <MessageList
                messages={messages}
                onRemoveMessage={this.onRemoveMessage}
              />
            ) : (
              <div>There are no messages ...</div>
            )}

            ...

          </div>
        )}
      </AuthUserContext.Consumer>
    );
  }
}
```

The MessageList component in between just pass the function through to the MessageItem component:

src/components/Home/index.js

```
const MessageList = ({ messages, onRemoveMessage }) => (
  <ul>
    {messages.map(message => (
      <MessageItem
        key={message.uid}
        message={message}
        onRemoveMessage={onRemoveMessage}
      />
    ))}
  </ul>
);
```

Finally it can be used in the MessageItem component. When clicking the button, we will pass the message identifier to the function. Then in our parent component that has access to Firebase we can remove the message associated with the identifier.

src/components/Home/index.js

```
const MessageItem = ({ message, onRemoveMessage }) => (
  <li>
    <strong>{message.userId}</strong> {message.text}
    <button
      type="button"
      onClick={() => onRemoveMessage(message.uid)}
    >
      Delete
    </button>
  </li>
);
```

Last, implement the class method that deletes the item from the list. Since we have access to the identifier of the message, we can use the reference of a single message to remove it.

src/components/Home/index.js

```
class MessagesBase extends Component {
  ...

  onRemoveMessage = uid => {
    this.props.firebase.message(uid).remove();
  };


  ...
}
```

Deleting a message works, and you can also make Firebase instance available to the MessageItem component and delete the message there right away. The real-time connection to the Firebase database in the Messages component would still be called to remove the message, which keeps the displayed messages in sync. However, aggregating all the business logic in one place, in this case the Messages component, makes sense for a better maintainability and predictability of the application. Only a few components have the more complex logic whereas the other components are just there to render the content.

Editing an Item in a List

It's abnormal to update a message in a chat application, but we'll implement this feature anyway. Eventually, we'll give other users feedback that a message was edited. That way, all statements made in the chat keep their integrity. Again, implement the class method first, which we will fill with details later, and pass it down to the MessageList component:

src/components/Home/index.js

```
class MessagesBase extends Component {
  ...

  onEditMessage = () => {
    ...
  };

  render() {
    const { text, messages, loading } = this.state;

    return (
      <AuthUserContext.Consumer>
        {authUser => (
          <div>
            ...

            {messages ? (
              <MessageList
                messages={messages}
                onEditMessage={this.onEditMessage}
                onRemoveMessage={this.onRemoveMessage}
              />
            ) : (
              <div>There are no messages ...</div>
            )}

            ...
          </div>
        )}
      </AuthUserContext.Consumer>
    );
  }
}
```

Again, the MessageList component just passes it through to the MessageItem component:

src/components/Home/index.js

```
const MessageList = ({
  messages,
  onEditMessage,
  onRemoveMessage,
}) => (
  <ul>
    {messages.map(message => (
      <MessageItem
        key={message.uid}
        message={message}
        onEditMessage={onEditMessage}
        onRemoveMessage={onRemoveMessage}
      />
    ))}
  </ul>
);
```

Editing a message involves a few more rendered elements, business logic, and state in the MessageItem component. That's why we refactor it to a class component:

src/components/Home/index.js

```
class MessageItem extends Component {
  ...
}
```

Next, we'll keep track of the mode of the component, which tells us if we're showing the text of a message or editing it. Also, if we are editing a message, we need to track the value of the input field element. As initial state, it receives the text of the message entity which makes sense if we only want to edit a typo in the message:

src/components/Home/index.js

```
class MessageItem extends Component {
    constructor(props) {
      super(props);

      this.state = {
        editMode: false,
        editText: this.props.message.text,
      };
    }


    . . .
}
```

Now, let's implement three class methods, the first of which is a class method for toggling the mode from edit to preview and back. If this mode is toggled, we always fill in the text of the message as a value for the input field element to improve the user experience when the mode is toggled:

src/components/Home/index.js

```
class MessageItem extends Component {
    . . .

  onToggleEditMode = () => {
    this.setState(state => ({
      editMode: !state.editMode,
      editText: this.props.message.text,
    }));
  };


    . . .
}
```

Second, a class method for updating the value in the input field:

src/components/Home/index.js

```
class MessageItem extends Component {
  ...

  onChangeEditText = event => {
    this.setState({ editText: event.target.value });
  };

  ...
}
```

And third, a class method to submit the final value to the parent component to edit the message:

src/components/Home/index.js

```
class MessageItem extends Component {
  ...

  onSaveEditText = () => {
    this.props.onEditMessage(this.props.message, this.state.editText);

    this.setState({ editMode: false });
  };

  ...
}
```

Later, we will see why we send the message with the edited text. Next, let's implement the render method of the MessageItem component. Make sure that the button to delete a message is not displayed in edit mode:

src/components/Home/index.js

```
class MessageItem extends Component {
  ...

  render() {
    const { message, onRemoveMessage } = this.props;
    const { editMode, editText } = this.state;

    return (
      <li>
        <span>
```

```
      <strong>{message.userId}</strong> {message.text}
    </span>

    {!editMode && (
      <button
        type="button"
        onClick={() => onRemoveMessage(message.uid)}
      >
        Delete
      </button>
    )}
  </li>
);
}
}
```

Next add "Edit" and "Reset" buttons to toggle between preview and edit mode. Depending on the edit mode, the correct button is displayed, and a "Save" button is shown in edit mode to save the edited text:

src/components/Home/index.js

```
class MessageItem extends Component {
  ...

  render() {
    const { message, onRemoveMessage } = this.props;
    const { editMode, editText } = this.state;

    return (
      <li>
        <span>
          <strong>{message.userId}</strong> {message.text}
        </span>

        {editMode ? (
          <span>
            <button onClick={this.onSaveEditText}>Save</button>
            <button onClick={this.onToggleEditMode}>Reset</button>
          </span>
        ) : (
          <button onClick={this.onToggleEditMode}>Edit</button>
        )}
```

```
      . . .
    </li>
  );
  }
}
```

Last, we need the input field element to edit the text. It is only displayed in edit mode. If we are not in edit mode, the actual text of the message is shown:

src/components/Home/index.js

```
class MessageItem extends Component {
  . . .

  render() {
    const { message, onRemoveMessage } = this.props;
    const { editMode, editText } = this.state;

    return (
      <li>
        {editMode ? (
          <input
            type="text"
            value={editText}
            onChange={this.onChangeEditText}
          />
        ) : (
          <span>
            <strong>{message.userId}</strong> {message.text}
          </span>
        )}

        . . .
      </li>
    );
  }
}
```

Now we can edit the text in edit mode, and we can also reset the whole thing using a button. If we save the edited text, the text and the message will be sent through the MessageList component to the Messages component, where the message can be identified by id to be edited with the text property. Using the spread operator, all other properties of the message entity are kept as before:

src/components/Home/index.js

```
class MessagesBase extends Component {
  ...

  onEditMessage = (message, text) => {
    const { uid, ...messageSnapshot } = message;

    this.props.firebase.message(message.uid).set({
      ...messageSnapshot,
      text,
    });
  };

  ...
}
```

If we set only the new text for the message, all other properties (e.g. userId) would be lost. Also we can add createdAt and editedAt dates. The second date gives users feedback that someone changed a chat message:

src/components/Home/index.js

```
class MessagesBase extends Component {
  ...

  onCreateMessage = (event, authUser) => {
    this.props.firebase.messages().push({
      text: this.state.text,
      userId: authUser.uid,
      createdAt: this.props.firebase.serverValue.TIMESTAMP,
    });

    this.setState({ text: '' });

    event.preventDefault();
  };

  onEditMessage = (message, text) => {
    const { uid, ...messageSnapshot } = message;

    this.props.firebase.message(message.uid).set({
      ...messageSnapshot,
      text,
```

```
      editedAt: this.props.firebase.serverValue.TIMESTAMP,
    });
  };


  ...

}
```

When using Firebase, it's best not to choose the date yourself, but let Firebase choose it depending on their internal mechanics. The server value constants from Firebase can be made available in the Firebase class:

src/components/Firebase/firebase.js

```
class Firebase {
  constructor() {
    app.initializeApp(config);

    /* Helper */

    this.serverValue = app.database.ServerValue;
    this.emailAuthProvider = app.auth.EmailAuthProvider;


    ...

  }


  ...

}
```

In the MessageItem component, give users feedback that shows when a message was edited:

src/components/Home/index.js

```
class MessageItem extends Component {
  ...

  render() {
    const { message, onRemoveMessage } = this.props;
    const { editMode, editText } = this.state;

    return (
      <li>
        {editMode ? ( ... ) : (
          <span>
            <strong>{message.userId}</strong> {message.text}
```

```
        {message.editedAt && <span>(Edited)</span>}
      </span>
    )}


    ...

  </li>
);
}
}
```

As before, we could have used Firebase directly in the MessageItem component. It's also good to keep the MessageItem component encapsulated with its own business logic. Only the message itself and the other functions to alter the message are passed from above to the component, and only the Messages component speaks to the outside world (e.g. Firebase).

You have implemented the popular CRUD operations: create, read, update, delete, which is everything you need to manage the new message entity in your Firebase database. Also, you have learned how to assign dates to your Firebase entities, and how to listen for real-time updates when a message has been added, edited or removed.

Securing User Interactions

So far, every user can edit and remove messages. Let's change this by giving only owner of messages the power to perform these operations within the UI. Therefore, we need the authenticated user in the MessageItem component. Since we already have the authenticated user in the Messages component, let's pass it down to the MessageList component:

src/components/Home/index.js

```
class MessagesBase extends Component {

  ...

  render() {
    const { text, messages, loading } = this.state;
    return (
      <AuthUserContext.Consumer>
        {authUser => (
          <div>

            ...

            {messages ? (
              <MessageList
                authUser={authUser}
                messages={messages}
                onEditMessage={this.onEditMessage}
                onRemoveMessage={this.onRemoveMessage}
              />
            ) : (
              <div>There are no messages ...</div>
            )}

            ...

          </div>
        )}
      </AuthUserContext.Consumer>
    );
  }
}
```

And from there down to the MessageItem component:

src/components/Home/index.js

```
const MessageList = ({
  authUser,
  messages,
  onEditMessage,
  onRemoveMessage,
}) => (
  <ul>
    {messages.map(message => (
      <MessageItem
        authUser={authUser}
        key={message.uid}
        message={message}
        onEditMessage={onEditMessage}
        onRemoveMessage={onRemoveMessage}
      />
    ))}
  </ul>
);
```

Now in your MessageItem component, you can secure the buttons to edit and remove messages by comparing the message's userId with the authenticated user's id:

src/components/Home/index.js

```
class MessageItem extends Component {
  ...

  render() {
    const { authUser, message, onRemoveMessage } = this.props;
    const { editMode, editText } = this.state;

    return (
      <li>
        ...

        {authUser.uid === message.userId && (
          <span>
            {editMode ? (
              <span>
                <button onClick={this.onSaveEditText}>Save</button>
                <button onClick={this.onToggleEditMode}>Reset</button>
              </span>
```

```
      ) : (
        <button onClick={this.onToggleEditMode}>Edit</button>
      )}
      {!editMode && (
        <button
          type="button"
          onClick={() => onRemoveMessage(message.uid)}
        >
          Delete
        </button>
      )}
    </span>
  )}
  </li>
  );
  }
}
```

That's it for only enabling users who are owners of a message to edit and delete the message in the UI. You will see later how you can secure the Firebase API endpoint as well to not allow users to edit/delete entities; otherwise it would still be possible to alter the source code in the browser to show the buttons for deleting and editing messages even though the user has no permission to perform it.

Ordering

Currently, messages are retrieved in no specific order from the Firebase realtime database, which means they would be in the order of their creation. This is appropriate for a chat application, but let's make this behavior more explicit by ordering them by the `createdAt` date property since we have introduced this earlier:

src/components/Home/index.js

```
class MessagesBase extends Component {

  ...

  componentDidMount() {
    this.setState({ loading: true });

    this.props.firebase
      .messages()
      .orderByChild('createdAt')
      .on('value', snapshot => {
        const messageObject = snapshot.val();

        ...
      });
  }

  ...

}
```

Pass the property that should be used to retrieved the list as ordered list from the Firebase realtime database. By default Firebase is ordering the items in ascending direction. To reverse the order, add a `reverse()` after transforming the list of messages from an object to an array.

You might see a warning about indexing data in Firebase's realtime database, because we're fetching data in a specific order, and Firebase uses the property `createdAt` to fetch it more efficiently. You can index messages using the `createdAt` property to give Firebase a performance boost when fetching the messages with this ordering. Head over to your project's Firebase dashboard, open the "Database" tab, and click the "Rules" tab. You can add the indexing of the data there:

Firebase Dashboard -> Databasse Tab -> Rules Tab

```json
{
  "rules": {
    "messages": {
      ".indexOn": ["createdAt"]
    }
  }
}
```

The warning should no longer appear, and Firebase became faster at retrieving messages by creation date. Every time you see the warning popping up, head over to your rules and index your Firebase entities. It makes your Firebase database operations faster.

Pagination

Next is the ordering feature, and we will paginate the list from the Firebase realtime database as well. You can pass the Firebase API a limit method with an integer to specify how many items you are interested in:

src/components/Home/index.js

```
class MessagesBase extends Component {

  ...

  componentDidMount() {
    this.setState({ loading: true });

    this.props.firebase
      .messages()
      .orderByChild('createdAt')
      .limitToLast(5)
      .on('value', snapshot => {
        ...
      });
  }


  ...

}
```

Limiting the items is half the task for enabling pagination for our chat application. We also need to move the limit to the local state of the component to adjust it later with user interactions to fetch more than five items:

src/components/Home/index.js

```
class MessagesBase extends Component {
  constructor(props) {
    super(props);

    this.state = {
      text: '',
      loading: false,
      messages: [],
      limit: 5,
    };
  }
```

```
componentDidMount() {
  this.setState({ loading: true });

  this.props.firebase
    .messages()
    .orderByChild('createdAt')
    .limitToLast(this.state.limit)
    .on('value', snapshot => {
      ...
    });
}


...

}
```

Move this functionality outside of the lifecycle method to make it reusable for other user interaction, and to use it outside of when the component mounts:

src/components/Home/index.js

```
class MessagesBase extends Component {
  ...

  componentDidMount() {
    this.onListenForMessages();
  }

  onListenForMessages() {
    this.setState({ loading: true });

    this.props.firebase
      .messages()
      .orderByChild('createdAt')
      .limitToLast(this.state.limit)
      .on('value', snapshot => {
        ...
      });
  }

  ...
}
```

Next, let's add a button to indicate that we are interested in more than five items:

src/components/Home/index.js

```
class MessagesBase extends Component {
  ...

  onNextPage = () => {
    this.setState(
      state => ({ limit: state.limit + 5 }),
      this.onListenForMessages,
    );
  };

  render() {
    const { text, messages, loading } = this.state;

    return (
      <AuthUserContext.Consumer>
        {authUser => (
          <div>
            {!loading && messages && (
              <button type="button" onClick={this.onNextPage}>
                More
              </button>
            )}

            ...

          </div>
        )}
      </AuthUserContext.Consumer>
    );
  }
}
```

The button uses a new class method that increases the limit by five again. Afterward, using the second argument of React's setState method, we can renew the Firebase listener with the new limit from the local state. We know that the second function in this React-specific method runs when the asynchronous state update happens, at which point the listener can use the correct limit from the local state.

Everything you have learned in this chapter should make you proficient with structured and list data in Firebase's realtime database. You have learned how to get, create, update and remove entities in a Firebase realtime database, and how to keep a synchronized connection to Firebase and always show the latest entities. Finally, we went through the pagination and ordering features offered by Firebase.

Exercises:

- Read more about structuring data in Firebase[91]
- Read more about working with lists of data in Firebase[92]
- Read more about indexing your Firebase data[93]
- Confirm your source code for the last section[94]
- Refactoring:
    - Move all user related components on the AdminPage to their own folder/file module.
    - Move all message related components on the HomePage to their own folder/file module.
    - Confirm your source code for this refactoring[95]
- Prevent fetching more items with the "More" button when there are no more items available.

---

[91] https://firebase.google.com/docs/database/web/structure-data
[92] https://firebase.google.com/docs/database/web/lists-of-data
[93] https://firebase.google.com/docs/database/security/indexing-data
[94] http://bit.ly/2Vng1Sc
[95] http://bit.ly/2VplDLI

Firebase Hosting

After we built a full-fledged Firebase application in React, the final step is deployment, the tipping point of getting your ideas out into the world, from consuming tutorials to producing applications. Since you have already used Firebase extensively for your application, why not choosing Firebase Hosting for the deployment?

In this section, I want to guide you through deploying your React application to Firebase. It works for create-react-app too. Also it should work for any other library and framework such as Angular or Vue. First, install the Firebase CLI globally to your node modules:

Command Line

```
npm install -g firebase-tools
```

Using a global installation of the Firebase CLI, you can deploy any application without worrying about the dependency in your project. For any global installed node package, remember to update it occasionally to a newer version with the identical command:

Command Line

```
npm install -g firebase-tools
```

Next associate the Firebase CLI with a Firebase account (Google account):

Command Line

```
firebase login
```

There should be a URL in your command line that opens in a browser. If this doesn't happen, Firebase CLI may open up the URL automatically. Choose your Google account you used earlier to create a Firebase project, and give Google the necessary permissions. You should see a confirmation for a successful setup. Return to the command line to verify a successful login.

Next, move to the project's folder and execute the following command, which initializes a Firebase project that can be used for the Firebase hosting features:

Command Line

```
firebase init
```

Then, choose the Hosting option. If you are interested in using another tool to host your Firebase application, choose another option:

Command Line

```
? Which Firebase CLI features do you want to setup for this folder? Press Space to s\
elect features, then Enter to confirm your choices.
 ☐ Database: Deploy Firebase Realtime Database Rules
 ☐ Firestore: Deploy rules and create indexes for Firestore
 ☐ Functions: Configure and deploy Cloud Functions
☐☐ Hosting: Configure and deploy Firebase Hosting sites
 ☐ Storage: Deploy Cloud Storage security rules
```

Since Google knows about Firebase projects associated with your account after logged in, you are able to select your Firebase project from a list of projects from the Firebase platform:

Command Line

```
First, let's associate this project directory with a Firebase project.
You can create multiple project aliases by running firebase use --add,
but for now we'll just set up a default project.

? Select a default Firebase project for this directory:
-> react-firebase-authentic-d12f8 (react-firebase-authentication)
i  Using project react-firebase-authentic-d12f8 (react-firebase-authentication)
```

There are a few other configuration steps to define. Instead of using the default *public/* folder, we want to use the *build/* folder for create-react-app. If you set up the bundling with a tool like Webpack, you can choose the appropriate name for the build folder:

Command Line

```
? What do you want to use as your public directory? build
? Configure as a single-page app (rewrite all urls to /index.html)? Yes
? File public/index.html already exists. Overwrite? No
```

The create-react-app application creates a *build/* folder after you perform the `npm run build` for the first time. There you will find all the merged content from the *public/* folder and the *src/* folder. Since it is a single page application, we want to redirect the user always to the *index.html* file. From there React Router takes over for the client-side routing.

Now your Firebase initialization is complete. This step created a few configuration files for Firebase Hosting in your project's folder. You can read more about them in Firebase's documentation[96] for configuring redirects, a 404 page, or headers. Finally, deploy your React application with Firebase on the command line:

---

[96]https://firebase.google.com/docs/hosting/full-config

Command Line

```
firebase deploy
```

After a successful deployment, you should see a similar output with your project's identifier:

Command Line

```
Project Console: https://console.firebase.google.com/project/react-firebase-authenti\
c-d12f8/overview
Hosting URL: https://react-firebase-authentic-d12f8.firebaseapp.com
```

Visit both pages to observe the results. The former link navigates to your Firebase project's dashboard. There, you should have a new panel for the Firebase Hosting. The latter link navigates to your deployed React application.

If you only see a blank page for your deployed React application, see if the public key/value pair in the *firebase.json* is set to build. That's the case if your build folder has the name *build*. If it has another name, set the value to this. Second, check if you have ran the build script of your React app with npm run build. After you have done both steps, try another deployment with firebase deploy. That should get your recent React build up and running for Firebase Hosting.

Exercises

- Add the security rules from the installation instructions[97] to your Firebase Project's Dashboard for your Database.
- Read more about Firebase Hosting Features[98]
- Read more about how to host with Firebase Hosting[99]
- Connect your domain to your Firebase deployed application[100]

---

[97]https://github.com/the-road-to-react-with-firebase/react-firebase-authentication
[98]https://firebase.google.com/docs/hosting/
[99]https://firebase.google.com/docs/hosting/quickstart
[100]https://firebase.google.com/docs/hosting/custom-domain

How to continue your Journey ...

The Learning Pyramid[101] shows the relation between retention rates and mental activities, proving usable data for both teaching and learning. It is one of the most effective ways to measure lessons I have encountered since I started teaching programming. This is how typical mental activities break down according to retention rates:

- 5% Lecture
- 10% Reading
- 20% Audiovisual
- 30% Demonstration
- 50% Discussion
- 75% Practice by Doing
- 90% Teach Others

At the start of this book I mentioned that very few people can master programming by reading a book, and throughout I have emphasized applying the lessons as the best way to retain them. As you can see, teaching others has the biggest return on investment. I had the same experience when I started writing about web development, answered questions on Quora, Reddit, Stack Overflow, and wrote books. Teaching others forces you to dive deeper into topics, so you learn about the nuances of programming. Think of friends, coworkers, or online peers who want to learn about your lessons learned from this book. Both mentor and student can grow from the experience.

What's next after you have finished this book? So far, the book has taught you how to use Firebase in React to build modern web applications. You've used all the fundamental features to power your application with authentication, authorization, and database interaction. However, there is plenty of room to explore the ecosystem, starting with this book's exercises and articles.

Firebase's Cloud Firestore

Firebase's Cloud Firestore is the latest version of Firebase's Realtime Database. We used Realtime Database because it comes with plenty of documentation, has a more established community, and offers a lot of online tutorials. However, Firebase's Cloud Firestore might take over at some point, because it has a more intuitive data model, more features, faster queries, and a better scaling experience for larger applications. Since it only affects the Firebase database, everything else like the Firebase authentication mechanisms stays the same. You only need to migrate to Cloud Firestore[102] to give it a shot.

---

[101]https://www.google.com/search?q=learning+pyramid
[102]https://www.robinwieruch.de/react-firestore-tutorial

Firebase's Admin API

We used Firebase's authentication and realtime database in this book. Conversely, Firebase's admin API gives advanced control over users by changing email addresses, sending verification emails, or deleting them. As developer and admin, you are responsible for crafting a full-fledged admin dashboard to manage user entities without boundaries.

Firebase's Storage API

Firebase enables you to store files as well. For instance, users who have signed in to your application with a social login already come with an avatar, because they often use an image of themselves on Google, Facebook or Twitter. With Firebase's storage API, you can allow them to upload personalized profile pictures. It's may be also helpful for users who sign up with a email/password combination, because they will not have a profile picture in the first place. Give your users an option to upload images and explore the Firebase Storage API.

Firebase's Cloud Functions

Firebase's Cloud Functions are another advanced tool to outsource business logic from your application. For instance, cloud functions are often used to send recurring emails to users. When a user doesn't sign in for a while to your application, you could send this user a reminder email about the latest features they are missing out. Also you could use the cloud function to send emails about new content in your application. Exploring these email features with Firebase's Cloud Functions and Sendgrid[103] is a great learning experience in my opinion, because it let's you step away from only building frontend applications.

Stripe and PayPal

You can also enable payments for your Firebase in React application to make it a full-fledged business application. Stripe[104] and PayPal[105] are two platforms that add monetization, for actions like charging users a one-time fee or adding recurring subscriptions. This is the next step in building a profitable online service.

Keep Tinkering

The foremost recommendation I have is to continue tinkering with the React with Firebase application that you built in this book; as it's an ideal starter kit to realize your own ideas. As mentioned, you are free to substitute the technologies used under the hood, but maybe just focus on the features of your application. Since the user management is implemented for you, you can start

---

[103]https://sendgrid.com/
[104]https://www.robinwieruch.de/react-express-stripe-payment/
[105]https://www.robinwieruch.de/react-paypal-payment/

to add your own features from there. If you want to substitute Firebase with your own database and authentication, my other book The Road to GraphQL shows how too add these same features with your own backend application.

Thank You

Foremost, I want to thank you for reading this book or taking the full course. My greatest wishes are that you had a great learning experience with the material. I hope you enjoyed reading the book and I hope it helped you to gain some traction in this field of expertise. If you liked the book, your review on Amazon or Goodreads would mean the world to me.

Visit my website[106] to find more topics about software engineering and web development. I also have updates available by subscription[107]. If you liked the book, feel free to share it with anyone who might be interested in the topic. It should be used as giveaway for anyone who is striving to grow as a developer.

Thanks for reading, Robin.

---

[106]https://www.robinwieruch.de/
[107]https://www.getrevue.co/profile/rwieruch

Made in the USA
Middletown, DE
23 November 2019